TRUGGLE OR STARVE

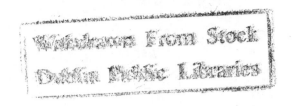

STRUGGLE OR STARVE

Working-Class Unity in Belfast's 1932 Outdoor Relief Riots

by Seán Mitchell

Foreword by Brian Kelly

Haymarket Books
Chicago, Illinois

Published in 2017 by
Haymarket Books
P.O. Box 180165
Chicago, IL 60618
773-583-7884
www.haymarketbooks.org
info@haymarketbooks.org

ISBN: 978-1-60846-678-8

Trade distribution:
In the US, Consortium Book Sales and Distribution, www.cbsd.com
In Canada, Publishers Group Canada, www.pgcbooks.ca
In the UK, Turnaround Publisher Services, www.turnaround-uk.com
All other countries, Ingram Publisher Services International,
intlsales@perseusbooks.com

This book was published with the generous support of Lannan Foundation
and Wallace Action Fund.

Cover design by Rachel Cohen. Cover image: Belfast Central Mission in 1932
organized to feed the children of the unemployed. Courtesy of Belfast Central
Mission Archive. Special thanks to Wesley Weir

Printed in Canada by union labor.

Library of Congress Cataloging-in-Publication data is available.

10 9 8 7 6 5 4 3 2 1

CONTENTS

To the memories of Bobby McCartan and Joe Johnny Rua.
I ndil cuimhne.

GLOSSARY
OF ORGANIZATIONS

Belfast Trades Council: Also known as the Belfast & District Trades Union Council. The council brings together representatives from trade unions from across Belfast.

Board of Guardians: An organization set up in the 1840s to oversee the Irish Poor Laws. The Guardians were elected by ratepayers and were tasked with the administration of the workhouses and the allocation of indoor and outdoor relief.

B-Specials: The Ulster Special Constabulary, composed of the A-Specials and the B-Specials, was Northern Ireland's quasi-paramilitary reserve police force, set up in October 1920, shortly before the partition of Ireland. Overwhelmingly Protestant in membership, the A-Specials were abolished in 1920. Disbandment of the B-Specials was one of the central demands of the modern civil rights movement. They were abolished in May 1970.

Irish Republican Army (IRA): An armed republican organization, dedicated to the ending of partition and the creation of an Irish Republic.

Nationalist Party: A mainly Catholic political party, formed by members of the Irish Parliamentary Party who were based in Northern Ireland. It had a number of members elected to the Northern Ireland Parliament and was led by Joe Devlin until 1934, when he was replaced by Thomas Joseph Campbell.

Northern Ireland Labour Party (NILP): A political party set up in 1924, linked to the trade unions. Prominent NILP figures in the 1930s included Jack Beattie and Harry Midgley.

Outdoor Relief Workers Committee (ODRWC): A committee set up on July 25, 1932, by Communists to organize those workers on Outdoor

Relief schemes.

Republican Congress: An Irish republican and socialist political organization founded in 1934, including left-wing elements who had split from the IRA and the Communist Party of Ireland. Key figures in the group were Peadar O'Donnell, Frank Ryan, and George Gilmore. The Congress dissolved in 1936.

Revolutionary Workers Groups (RWGs): A small Irish Communist grouping, formed in 1930 with the backing of the Soviet Union and its international network, the Comintern. It produced a paper, *Irish Workers' Voice* (later *Workers' Voice*), and was led by Seán Murray. Key RWG figures in Belfast included Tommy Geehan and Betty Sinclair. The group was renamed the Communist Party of Ireland in 1933.

Royal Ulster Constabulary (RUC): The largely Protestant police force in Northern Ireland, founded on June 1, 1922, out of the Royal Irish Constabulary.

Ulster Protestant League (UPL): A loyalist organization set up in 1931 to "safeguard the employment of Protestants." The UPL opposed any unity between Catholics and Protestants and in 1931 attacked an unemployment march organized by the RWGs. It produced a newspaper, *Ulster Protestant*, which carried the slogan "Vote Protestant, Buy Protestant, Sell Protestant, Be Protestant."

Ulster Unionist Party: The largest political party in Northern Ireland in 1932. Its origins can be traced back to the Ulster Unionist Council, formed in 1905. The party was led by James Craig during the 1930s, who was also the prime minister of Northern Ireland.

FOREWORD

by Brian Kelly

A lthough the bare essentials of the extraordinary upheaval at the core of this study are familiar to trade union and working-class activists in Belfast and throughout Ireland, it is a revealing fact that until now the 1932 Outdoor Relief (ODR) Strike has never been the subject of serious, extended treatment.[1] This is especially remarkable when we consider the vast literature that has grown up around the armed conflict that dominated life here in the closing decades of the last century, known euphemistically as "the Troubles." Journalists from across the globe have dissected the causes and effects of this violence, with rare exception settling upon the banal tautology that Northern Ireland's warring "religious tribes" could not help themselves from being drawn into an extended bout of reciprocal slaughter. University-based sociologists, political scientists, and historians have offered up only a slightly more sophisticated rendering, straining to absolve imperial rulers and regional elites from culpability in setting the context for sectarian antagonism, insisting that the most recent chapter in Belfast's long tragedy was driven by "ethno-religious" or "ethno-national" divisions that are essentially timeless and immutable, almost compulsive.

The conspicuous omission of the ODR strike from the narrative of Belfast's twentieth-century history demands an explanation, and although a detailed critique of the relevant historiography is not feasible here, it is possible to identify some of its main problems and in the process highlight the scale of what Seán Mitchell has managed to achieve in this important study. The absence of a serious examination of these events is part of a more general neglect of Belfast's rich labor history. James Connolly's mission, in *Labour in Irish History*, to "repair the deliberate neglect of the social question by our historians" is a task that remains unfinished in relation to Belfast, the "heartland of industrial capitalism in Ireland."[2] Although the city's modern evolution is intricately bound up with the linen mills and shipyards, the docks, ropeworks, tobacco factories, and large engineering enterprises that formed the basis of its economy, we have almost no mature historical literature on the working class whose labor made Belfast—for a time—an industrial powerhouse in the global economy.

The development of religious sectarianism as an enduring feature of life in the city is incomprehensible without some grasp of the relationship between the decline of rural northeastern Ulster, the pull of wage labor in industrializing Belfast, and the desperate competition generated by rapid, large-scale migration into a city in which Protestant men exercised an early monopoly over better-paid skilled labor, but no major study offers a broad, holistic analysis of this dynamic.[3] Belfast's 1907 Dockers' Strike ranks, alongside the 1913 Dublin Lockout, as one of the two most important industrial confrontations in Irish history, and yet it wasn't until the mid-1980s that it received serious attention—not at the hands of a professionally trained historian, as one might expect, but from an erudite veteran of the modern Irish civil rights and anti-internment movements.[4] The city's 1919 engineering strike—one of the most significant confrontations between labor and capital in post–World War I Ireland—serves as a test case in an extended study of unionist ideology among Protestant workers, figures tangentially in a wider exploration of revolutionary upheaval in Ireland, and receives minor treatment in a broad study of Irish syndicalism but has never been judged to merit the kind of sustained focus it deserves.[5] For the linen industry, involving mainly low-paid women workers, the situation is even more bleak: unpaid local historians, folk musicians, balladeers, and playwrights have performed a vital service in retrieving and preserving the "heritage" of the mills. For an industry that was central to the lives of so many of Belfast's working-class citizens on both sides of the sectarian divide, however, the absence of a single substantial study should be a cause for embarrassment.[6]

The turn in recent years to celebrating Belfast's industrial heritage as part of a "rebranding" project aimed at attracting tourism and multinational investment has not improved this dire situation. Driven forward by neoliberal advocates of privatization and free market ideology, the Titanic museum (the post-conflict city's signature development project) and the wider attempt to market a "re-imaged" Belfast purged of the traces of recent conflict has been framed as a celebration of the "captains of industry" and a paean to the city's entrepreneurial traditions. The new development has allowed some room for the "sights and sounds" of the shipyards but no real sense of the explosive class conflict or deep social inequalities that marked industrial Belfast.[7]

These gaps and silences partly reflect the long-term dominance of an especially conservative capitalist elite over regional politics. Throughout the latter half of the nineteenth century and for most of the twentieth those in command of local industry were universally tied to unionist politics (and often to the Orange Order), although in the "new" Belfast there seems to have developed a more ecumenical approach, with prominent nationalists attempting to outdo their counterparts in offering up eulogies to the market, and with foreign investors playing a much more prominent role in the local economy. Far from evidencing a determination to uproot sectarianism, this new, neoliberal Northern Ireland seems unable to move beyond superficial attempts to cover it over and keep it out of the global news cycle. When in June 2013 British prime minister David Cameron hosted a meeting of G8 leaders at a bankrupt hotel resort in Fermanagh, summit organizers hired a team of decorators to paint lively retail scenes over boarded-up shop windows in adjacent towns to impress the media throng with Northern Ireland's new prosperity. A few miles distant, a £75 million security operation saw 9,000 police drafted in from across the UK to erect a "ring of steel" aimed at preventing peaceful protesters from intruding on a gathering of rulers committed to imposing vicious austerity.[8] Together, Cameron's cheap stunt and the exorbitant outlay for repression epitomize the shallowness of the elite commitment to change. In sharp contrast to the determined and militant working-class unity on display during the ODR strike, the rebranding team in charge of post-conflict Belfast offers up whimsical solutions to enduring antagonism: in recent years city promoters have sought the solution to sectarianism in ice hockey, tall ships, and Twitter—to name but a few of the more serious campaigns.[9] Farcical stuff.

At the level of ideas there seems to be another important factor reinforcing the neglect of Belfast's working-class history. An often contentious but potentially fruitful debate has emerged in recent years over the impact of the Troubles on the writing of modern Irish history. This has mainly concerned the degree to which the emergence of violence in the North helped to cohere an exceptionally conservative and anti-republican consensus among mainstream journalists, public intellectuals, and university-based historians in Ireland, with their bias reflected in the relentless denigration of extra-constitutional and anti-imperialist forces in modern Irish history. John Newsinger, a British-based socialist historian then working on the mid-nineteenth-century Fenian movement, offered a measured critique of the trends evident in Irish historical writing between the mid-1970s and the turn of the new century. While acknowledging perfectly legitimate reasons—even an urgent imperative—to challenge the simplistic, nationalist rendering of Ireland's past, Newsinger characterized the revisionist thrust of recent historiography as "an essentially conservative project that seems almost always to endorse the moderate against the popular, the establishment against the rebel, evolution against revolution."[10]

In recent years this debate has sometimes focused intensely on differing interpretations of specific episodes during the Irish War of Independence, and even, at times, on readings and counter-readings of individual documents. Some of this is necessary, of course, for teasing out the truth, but in this close focus on detail we perhaps lose sight of the broader implications of the intense politicization of historical writing brought on by protracted crisis in the North. Significantly, Ireland's retreat into a conservative orthodoxy coincided with a dynamic turn toward "history from below" and an attempt to recover the "hidden transcripts of resistance" across much of the rest of the world. In Britain and the United States, for example, young scholars entering their studies fresh from the social upheavals of the 1960s turned their attention to exploring popular movements and often to excavating working-class history and recovering attempts by the most marginalized to remake society. Part of the larger explanation for why we have such an undeveloped literature on the Belfast working class may lie in the fact that, in its reaction against popular insurgency and, a few years later, an outbreak of protracted armed conflict that threatened stability, the Irish establishment—North and South—was moving in the opposite direction. With the struggle over the past as a key battleground, academics and public intellectuals were drawn into a rearguard defense of the status quo. If the re-stabilization delivered in the Belfast Agreement has dampened the urgency of that project, a new approach better suited to shoring up communal power-sharing constantly seeks the middle ground and "elevates sitting on the fence to an art form." In "its eagerness not to rehash what are seen as sterile debates concerning political violence," Brian Hanley has observed, "sometimes taking a position is abandoned altogether."[11]

Finally, the history of the ODR strike not only fits uncomfortably with elite renderings of the city's past; it challenges loyalist and republican worldviews as well. The story that Seán Mitchell reconstructs here is one that will sit awkwardly with many readers, in part because it offers little in the way of vindication for any of the main political tendencies operating in Belfast today. Beyond that, while it recounts an important episode in the city's history, the story of how organizers managed to achieve such an impressive degree of unity between Protestant and Catholic workers in a city built on sectarianism is one that defies any notion of smooth and steady progress. The Bible may be the only place where scales drop, instantaneously, from the eyes of the unseeing and their sight is restored. In the real world progress is more untidy: clarity and the confidence to act upon it comes to ordinary people as part of a more uneven and contradictory process. As Mitchell demonstrates convincingly and in vivid detail in the impressive study that follows, this was the case in Belfast during the depths of the last great crisis of global capitalism, and it is difficult to see how any future challenge to power in this city could take shape differently.

Brian Kelly
March 2017

INTRODUCTION

I well remember the beginning of that struggle. A mere handful of lads met in Unity Hall in North Street, to discuss the question of what was to be done to improve the lot of the Relief Workers in Belfast. From that small crowd we managed to get going one of the mightiest and grandest movements that ever was recorded in the history of the working class in Belfast. From that we accomplished what the Trade Union Leaders were never able, in all their years to accomplish. We accomplished the unity of the Catholic and Protestant workers.

—Tommy Geehan, leader of the Belfast unemployed movement, on the Custom House Steps, December 5, 1932

F riedrich Nietzsche, the controversial nineteenth-century writer and theoretician, once advanced the unusual idea that life was governed by what he called the law of eternal recurrence. Society, Nietzsche proposed, operated on a perennial cycle—of progress and regression, regression and progress—doomed to entrap humanity forevermore. It was a gloomy and cynical perspective, typical of the German philosopher's morose and pessimistic outlook, and one that rarely gets much traction these days. In Belfast, however, Nietzsche's prognosis that history was stuck on the repeat button might well appear to observers to be eerily accurate.

It is not difficult to see why. The cycle of violent sectarian conflict that has plagued the city since its founding is well documented. From the English colonial plantations of the sixteenth and seventeenth centuries and the endemic violence that they instigated, to the expulsion and displacement of thousands of (mainly working-class and Catholic) people from their homes and workplaces in the pogroms of 1912

1

and 1920, through the burning of Bombay Street and the protracted period of violence known as "the Troubles" that followed, Belfast
would appear to be stuck in a pattern that endlessly repeats itself.[1]
"Year after year," Andrew Boyd writes, the divided workers of Belfast
"turned the overcrowded slums which were their homes, and the factories and shipyards where they spent most of their dreary lives into
scenes of fearful rioting and destruction."[2] The sectarianism that fuels
this recurring pattern of violent division continues to linger, and the
city remains divided by walls, both real and imagined—including the
notorious "peace walls" that segregate Catholic and Protestant districts. In 1998 the Belfast Agreement was signed, ostensibly ushering
in a new dawn that would bridge the gap between the two dominant
political traditions—nationalism and unionism—and lay the basis for
a "shared society." It has done nothing of the sort. Two decades after
the ceasefires, the North of Ireland remains as divided as ever. Today
there are more peace walls in the city than there were in 1998, and
the politics of Orange (Protestant) and Green (Catholic) continue to
dominate a local administration so crisis-prone that the term "failed
state" would seem to be a gross understatement.

Not everyone is a victim in this cycle of sectarian polarization.
Belfast is one of the most unequal cities in Europe. Indeed, as of
2014 there are more multimillionaires in Belfast than any other city
in the United Kingdom apart from London and oil-rich Aberdeen.[3]
Yet thousands of children in the North grow up in poverty, wages are invariably lower in Belfast than in cities in either Britain or
the South of Ireland, and exceptionally large numbers of people rely
on disability benefits, in part because of the brutal legacy of the
Troubles. The working class of the North, hampered by sectarian
hate (including among its own divided ranks) and too frequently
betrayed by a trade union leadership unwilling to consistently confront sectarianism, has for a long time ceded the political ground to
bigots and demagogues among the "respectable" classes. The more
divided the class has been, the less influence it has in shaping society
in Northern Ireland. And the more deprived and impoverished the
hardest-hit sections of the working class, the more prone they seem
to falling back into sectarian animosity. Thus the vicious cycle seems

to repeat itself—potentially into eternity.

If there is a single phenomenon that epitomizes Belfast's recurrent antagonisms, then it must be the sectarian riot. Virtually every summer—during the Orange Order's annual Twelfth of July celebrations—the city is engulfed by sectarian tension, frequently leading to violence on the streets, particularly in the "interface" areas between Protestant and Catholic districts. Despite the best efforts of the tourism industry to airbrush away the sectarianism intrinsic to the Twelfth and rebrand the Orange marches as wholesome family fun, the image of the sectarian riot continues to shape international perspectives on the region. Some may protest that this is a lopsided view; it is true that the riots are for the most part isolated and usually short-lived. But the mere fact that they continue to plunge the city into intermittent crisis some two decades after the supposed end of the Troubles suggests that the cycle of sectarian hatred has yet to be broken.

One could be forgiven, then, for assuming that these deep and bitter sectarian divisions are an immutable and permanent fact of life in Belfast. Indeed the outworking of the Belfast Agreement has created a sort of "benign apartheid"—a society in which the two main communities coexist in isolation from one another—and the message from the government is that the rest of us should learn to live with it. The Outdoor Relief campaign appears, at first glance, to confirm the immutability of sectarian divisions. After all, the centerpiece of this work is a riot, one that involved all the usual violence: mass mobilization in the streets, stone-throwing, barricade-building, and an armed response from the state. It entailed vicious and prolonged fighting that involved Catholics and Protestants, barricades at interface areas, attacks on persons and property, and even guns and murder. As we shall see, however, the riots of 1932 were of a very different nature than those the media is used to broadcasting across the globe in its coverage of Northern Ireland.

The backdrop for the story is a familiar one, and of a piece with developments elsewhere around the world during the same period: poverty, hunger, unemployment, and a cruel and unforgiving government administration that drove working people to a sharp break with normal political routines of parliamentary democracy. During the

Great Depression of the 1930s, the Northern Ireland economy had been decimated by the consequences of the Wall Street Crash in the United States. Thousands of Catholic and Protestant workers alike faced a future on the breadline. Those out of work were forced to sign on for Outdoor Relief (ODR), where they would work on labor schemes and receive a bare pittance in return. As the unemployment rate skyrocketed to 40 percent in 1932, the failure of the Unionist government to alleviate the plight of the unemployed was producing bitterness and outrage across the working class.

It was in this context that a relatively small and previously uninfluential organization of Communists grouped around the Revolutionary Workers Groups (RWGs) entered the fray. The Communists formed an unemployment committee that unionized those on the ODR scheme and provided a focal point for wider layers of unemployed workers, both Catholic and Protestant, to organize. Driven by an unmatched audacity and impressive determination, the committee organized mass demonstrations of the unemployed—some numbering in excess of sixty thousand—across the city. A strike of the ODR workers themselves was organized, leading Belfast's unemployed into direct confrontation with a hostile and somewhat panicked Unionist administration, which determined to revert to type and crush the movement with force. The plan backfired, and the ODR riots were born.

In October 1932, the streets of Belfast were gripped by widespread rioting that lasted the better part of a week. From the Green districts along the Falls Road to the adjacent Orange districts of the Shankill, thousands of unarmed demonstrators fought pitched battles against heavily armed police, who trundled through working-class districts in caged police cars topped with mounted machine guns. Unemployed workers—indeed, whole working-class communities with a long experience of street fighting—tore up the cobblestone streets, digging trenches and erecting barricades to hold off the police assault. The event became known as the Outdoor Relief Riot—one of a very few instances in which class sympathy managed to trump sectarian loyalties in a city famous for its divisions.

Sharply contrasting with the normal pattern of conflict in the city, these riots were neither caused by sectarian enmity nor dominated by unionist or Irish nationalist political thinking. Uniquely, the ODR riots were an extended series of street confrontations driven by proletarian concerns, with the harsh years of the Great Depression compelling working-class people on both sides of the traditional divide to struggle alongside one another to secure a better life. In form and logistics the riots were not fought along communal lines: thousands of Catholics and Protestants literally joined forces—traversing the sectarian geography of the city—in an extraordinary show of unity that brought the Unionist government to its knees.

This book is not the first attempt to tell the story of the ODR struggle. Perhaps the best known of these is Paddy Devlin's *Yes, We Have No Bananas: Outdoor Relief in Belfast, 1920–1939*.[4] Devlin was a prominent and experienced figure in politics in the North, having served as a Member of Parliament for the Northern Ireland Labour Party (NILP) and later becoming a founding member of the more nationalist-centered Social Democratic and Labour Party. His book combines a rigorous critique of the Irish Poor Laws, the legislation that governed the country's unemployed, with a passionate defense of the men and women who were subject to its punitive regime. Devlin shows how treatment of the unemployed was informed not by sympathy for their plight but by narrow political and sectarian considerations. His account of the unemployment movement of 1932 is extremely limited, however. In particular, Devlin pays scant regard to the actual dynamics of unemployed campaigning, telling us almost nothing about how the agitation arose or the political motivations spurring on the activists who drove it forward. As a result, Devlin's account depicts the ODR riots as little more than a spontaneous explosion of anger, ignoring the long campaign that preceded the upheaval and the Communist agitation that informed it. There is another problem with Devlin's book: in downplaying the militancy surrounding the ODR agitation, Devlin leaves the impression that the unemployed movement was a rather lighthearted and jocular affair, when in reality it was nothing of the sort. Even the most frequently referenced aspect of the book, its title, can be misleading: Devlin claims that "Yes, We Have No Bananas"—a well-known pop song at the time—was the only tune played at a demonstration of the unemployed, "to avoid giving religious offence."[5] It is possible that this song was played at one protest or more, but it is hardly the enduring legacy of 1932 and can be read as suggesting that the movement itself was a jovial, tame affair. The mood of the unemployed movement was much more militant and dynamic than Devlin would have us believe. The unemployed, in fact, had their own songs that they would sing while marching through the streets. And the banners on display throughout would suggest that avoiding giving offense was not always the most pressing priority for those who took part in the movement.

If Devlin's book is guilty of sanitizing the events of 1932, then Ronaldo Munck and Bill Rolston's *Belfast in the Thirties: An Oral History* goes some way to redressing the balance.[6] Based primarily on oral accounts of the period—collected by the authors more than forty years after the events—this book is both a scholarly collection of personal recollections from a range of activists and an intelligent and engaging exploration of the politics of Depression-era Belfast, peppered throughout with revealing insights into the life of working-class people and activists who helped shape the times. Munck and Rolston's study is a fine collection of retrospective oral accounts of the 1930s, but as a rounded analysis of the riots it falls far short. Partly this reflects the retrospective nature of the oral accounts themselves: the interviews were conducted some forty years after the events, and many of them are colored by the politics of the 1970s rather than the 1930s. One example will illustrate this. Leading Communist Betty Sinclair claims in her account that republicans played no role whatsoever in the event, a claim that is completely false and even contradicted by the internal documentation of the Communists themselves from the period. Likewise, her claim that the RWGs had close to a thousand members in Belfast is considerably off the mark, with the Communists at the time never publicly or privately claiming more than 120 members.[7] Sinclair is not alone in advancing this kind of self-serving revision. In order to separate the truth from this kind of willful misrepresentation of the past, it is necessary to combine oral recollections with a rigorous examination of all available documentary sources, as this study seeks to do.

There is another weakness in *Belfast in the Thirties*. The central premise of the book is that the "supposed class unity" of the ODR strike was not "unique, even in Belfast terms" and that "class and religion generated two forms of political practice with independent rhythms"—concluding that the entire event has been romanticized out of proportion by the Left and labor movement.[8] Certainly the relationship between class and sectarianism that the authors allude to here is complex, and my own attempt to explore this problem can be found in the concluding chapters. However, in dismissing the idea that working-class struggle can overcome sectarianism, Munck and Rolston have undoubtedly downplayed the significance of the events of 1932. This is a mistake now common across most accounts of the period. One historian chronicling the rise of the Irish Communist Party, for example, argues that "[t]he brief unity between Protestant and Catholic workers displayed during the strike came to an abrupt end in July due to violence from the RUC [Royal Ulster Constabulary, a militarised police force] and loyalists."[9] It is unclear precisely what violence the author is referring to here. Is this a reference to the violence that occurred the summer before the riots? Or perhaps the pogroms of the summer of 1935? In any case, such a narrow assessment of the impact of 1932 on Irish history will hardly suffice. Another historian, in this case undertaking a study of the Irish Republican Army (IRA) during the period, goes further, concluding that "the few radical Protestants [involved in the ODR riots] were quickly deserted by their following, leaving the 'Taigs' and the 'Fenians' vulnerable to the baton swinging RUC."[10] Not only is this rendering of the events wrong from a factual point of view, it downplays the significant degree of working-class unity achieved during this period and ignores the tangible, long-term impact the events had on the thinking of individuals involved in a range of political movements during the Depression years, including many republicans.

Most historians, therefore, have given short shrift to the events of 1932. Those that have paid any attention to the rising of Belfast's unemployed workers have tended to treat the episode with condescension, littering their remarks with generalizations about the starry-eyed, romantic myth of the ODR struggle. It is the contention of this study, however, that in countering a simplistic and romanticized folk memory of the events, academic historiography has created its own false mythology of the period—one that seriously underestimates the significance of the event. This work seeks to reassert the importance of the Outdoor Relief riots and the unemployment agitation of the 1930s in the narrative of twentieth-century Irish history. It argues that the crisis of 1932 was an event of seminal importance that rocked the establishment to its core and threw the whole of the political firmament into upheaval. For republicanism, the ODR riots were a significant turning point, inspiring dozens of activists to take up social questions and helping to precipitate a split in the movement that ushered in an important leftward turn reflected in the rise of the Republican Congress in 1934. For working-class Protestants too, the ODR strike was an event of profound importance. It was one of the few moments in the history of modern Belfast when the divide between rich and poor superseded the traditional separation dividing poor Catholics from poor Protestants. It was the moment when the myth of "Protestant privilege" was clearly exposed, as Protestant workers and the unemployed took to the streets alongside their Catholic workmates and neighbors to challenge the real privilege of Unionist elites.

There is no full appraisal of the riots of 1932, the events leading up to it, or its aftermath in print. This book seeks to fill that inexplicable void by building on the existing literature and combining it with a full use of a wide range of sources. Newspapers from the time, including those of unionist and nationalist persuasion, bear witness to the sheer scale of the crisis and provide extensive reports on demonstrations, riots, and the ideological offensive carried out in response. Detailed accounts of many of the unemployed meetings are found in RUC intelligence reports, which also convey state perceptions of the emerging movement and its changing tactics for dealing with the crisis. Communist papers provide a sense of the politics and activities of leading elements of the campaign, while internal documentation sent to the Comintern in Russia offers revealing insights into the internal machinations and perceptions of the organization as it moved over a matter of months from a position of obscurity to the head of a mass movement.

This study provides a detailed though critical account of the unemployment agitation of that year, explaining how the activity of local Communists acted as a driving force for the emergence of a mass movement of working-class Catholics and Protestants. Additionally, *Struggle or Starve* provides a blow-by-blow account of the ODR riots themselves, illuminating the asymmetrical confrontation between heavily armed state forces and the bedraggled but determined people opposing them. It reveals how Protestant workers came to the aid of a besieged and embattled Catholic community, providing the impetus for a citywide ferment that shook the state to its core. Finally, this book engages with the politics of the period and examines the complex relationship between class and sectarianism during and after the ODR struggle.

For most of its tumultuous history, the city of Belfast has seemed trapped in a perpetual cycle of division and violence, unable to escape the familiar rut of divisions between Orange and Green. But for a brief period during the depths of the Great Depression—a period marked by upheaval and unfamiliar possibilities—the red flag fluttered above non-sectarian, working-class-led demonstrations numbering in the tens of thousands; the streets of Belfast became convulsed with popular protest, and the eternal recurrence of Irish history was temporarily broken. This book, written as a contribution from someone anxious to play a role in carving out a future free from sectarianism, aims to tell the story of that remarkable moment in our past.

Chapter 1

THE CREATION
OF THE NORTHERN IRELAND STATE

T he state of Northern Ireland was the product of a dramatic
and profound Irish constitutional crisis in the period during
and after the First World War. The weakening British government found the continuation of its rule untenable, leading to heated
debate over home rule—the possibility of self-government within
Ireland, rather than direct colonial rule from England. Partition
provided the basis for an imperial solution to this crisis. In 1919
the British government announced its intention to create two parliaments in Ireland—one in six of the nine counties of Ulster—the
other in the remaining twenty-six counties.

The "Irish Question" had long been a source of political dispute and tension for British imperialism. Despite a number of
half-hearted attempts at its resolution through a series of botched
home rule bills, no answer could be found that was acceptable to
both the ruling class in London and the Irish people. The British
were reluctant to relinquish their hold over the country, fearing that
any concession to demands for Irish independence would inspire
similar demands throughout the empire. It was this global imperial
context that ultimately informed the response of the British state to
calls for an independent Ireland. They crushed the 1916 Easter Rising—a rebellion of some 1,300 republican and socialist insurgents
that sought to end British rule—with the full force of their military
might, dealing ruthlessly with those who partook in the rebellion by

executing sixteen of its leaders and interning 3,600 people, including many that were not involved in the Rising. Unfortunately for
the authorities in London, instead of crushing militant nationalism
this repression accelerated its growth and influence throughout the
country, transforming republicanism from a tight-knit conspiratori-
al grouping into a broadly supported national liberation movement.
The rise of the IRA as an effective guerrilla force, combined with the
emergence of a widespread campaign of resistance and civil disobe-
dience, forced the British to reevaluate their position in Ireland.

Any movement for independence, however, faced one significant difficulty, which the British government worked to exploit—
the militant opposition of Unionists in the Northeast of the country
to any break with the empire. Led by a number of powerful Protestant industrialists and by sections of the landed Irish aristocracy,
Unionist elites viewed the link between Ulster and the British Empire as a crucial component in maintaining the system of privilege
that underpinned their political and economic power. In particular,
they feared that independence would result in their isolation from
the far-flung markets of trade and commerce that had proven so
crucial in the expansion of industries like linen and shipbuilding. As
an Ulster Unionist Council report in 1911 succinctly put it, "Ulster
Unionists . . . have built up their industries and brought Ulster to
its present prosperous condition under the protection of the Imperial Parliament. . . . This position they are prepared to maintain
at all hazards."[1] Deep political alliances had developed alongside
these economic links—particularly between Ulster's elites, Britain's
Conservative Party, and influential elements in the British military
establishment—and this relationship was key to shaping British
policy in Ireland in favor of the Unionists.

Unionist elites also feared that independence would undermine
the political dominance that they had enjoyed in Ulster over many
years. Over the course of the nineteenth century they had skillfully
constructed a movement that served the rich and the powerful while
simultaneously claiming the allegiance of a significant section of the
Protestant working class. The "great strength of the Ulster Unionist
movement," according to one historian, "was that it embraced all so-

cial classes and had a mass base": this all-class alliance was formed in part through regular resorts to sectarianism, but it also depended on the institutionalization of a system of preference in employment and housing, backed by organizations like the Orange Order.[2] Through this process, unionism built up formidable links between Protestant workers and their employers, which proved effective in containing anti-establishment dissent in times of crisis. As insurance against the possibility that their links with the British establishment would not be enough to prevent the creation of an independent Ireland, Unionists set about creating a paramilitary organization that would violently resist any proposed change, culminating in the formation of the Ulster Volunteer Force in 1912. The close links between Ulster elites and British capitalism and the constant threat of violent resistance to any challenges ensured that no deal would be made over the heads of the Unionists, and republicans were in no position—either politically or militarily—to challenge unionism in the Northeast.

The anticolonial movement had proven itself to be a formidable foe for the British military in Ireland—expelling it from large swathes of the Irish countryside and disrupting its urban political operations—but it contained fundamental weaknesses that limited its scope as a project for radical social change. Republicanism was a largely middle class–led movement, whose appeal was primarily nationalist, limiting its attraction to the Protestant sections of the working class in Ulster and leaving the all-class alliance of unionism secure. This did not mean that republicanism and unionism were mirror images of each other: historically republicanism expressed a desire to break with the injustices that British rule had wrought in Ireland while unionism was determined to maintain them. Nor was republicanism afflicted with the kind of intrinsic sectarian rationale that underpinned unionism. After all, it was at its genesis a creation of radical Protestantism—the majority of the leadership of the United Irishmen, for example, were Presbyterians—and in contrast to the sectarian appeals of unionism, it was committed (verbally at least) to uniting the Irish people as a whole, "Catholic, Protestant and Dissenter." Despite this, republicanism failed to make any serious inroads into the Protestant population and was largely confined to the Catholic majority, leaving it susceptible to the Unionist critique of Irish independence as a reactionary Catholic ideal (giving rise to the political jab "Home Rule Equals Rome Rule"). This was a shortcoming that opponents of republicanism were eager to exploit.

Unionists skillfully combined scaremongering over independence with an assurance that the socioeconomic well-being of poorer Protestants would be assured through sectarian preference in the allocation of jobs and the security ostensibly afforded by inclusion in the empire. The republican movement, based as it was on appeals to nationalism, had only a limited ability to attract support from this section of the population, leaving the Unionist all-class alliance largely untouched—a case of "better the devil you know than the devil you don't," as James Connolly argued:

> When the Sinn Féiner speaks to men who are fighting against low wages and tells them that the body has promised lots of Irish labour at low wages to any foreign capitalist who wished to establish in Ireland, what wonder if they come to believe that a change from Toryism to Sinn Féinism would simply be a change from the devil they do know to the devil they do not.[3]

The only project that might have seriously undermined unionism was one that sought to win a section of Protestant workers to a vision of an Ireland freed not only from British domination but from sharp class inequality, a project that aimed directly at driving a wedge between ordinary Protestants and "big house" Unionists. The easy absorption of working-class Protestants into an elite-led sectarian alliance had never been without its complications: the movement had frequently been convulsed by an "undercurrent of lower-class resentment" against the landed and industrial elites who directed it.[4] At times this found expression in breakaway independent Unionist currents, most famously when Tom Sloan—an independent Unionist himself, with a base mainly among Protestant workers in the south of the city—took the Westminster seat for Belfast South from the Conservative Party in 1902, largely as a result of discontent with local Unionist bosses.[5] Independent Unionism did, at times, provide an outlet for working-class Protestant frustrations, though it rarely strayed very far from the project of cross-class unity at the heart of unionism, and despite its nuisance value usually fell in line behind Orange elites. But fissures within the Unionist project could also develop from a more explicitly Left direction: in periods of sharp class polarization, as during the 1907 Dockers' Strike and the 1919 Engineers' Strike, the Orange alliance had come under considerable strain.

The 1907 Belfast Dockers' Strike is, alongside the 1913 Dublin Lockout, the most celebrated struggle in the history of the Irish labor movement. Under the leadership of "Big Jim" Larkin, thousands of previously unorganized dockworkers resisted an attempt by employers to lock them out for daring to organize in a trade union. When employers attempted to break the strike with scab labor, the stoppage spread to local carters who refused to handle the goods emanating from the docks. Some two hundred thousand workers from across Belfast's sectarian divide marched in solidarity with the strike, and tensions even emerged within the ranks of the local police when hundreds of officers threatened mutiny. The significance of the working-class unity on display during the strike was not lost on Belfast's ruling class. Echoing the experience of the 1905 Revolution in Petrograd, one local newspaper, the *Northern Whig*, declared: "We are on the eve of an experience something akin to which has paralysed Russian cities during the last couple of years."[6] Alas, the trade union leadership in Britain did not quite have the stomach of those who led the 1905 Revolution: solidarity actions were called off, leaving the strike isolated and ultimately leading to its defeat.

What happened in 1907 was not an aberrant occurrence. In 1919, Belfast was again brought to a standstill as a result of a general strike demanding the introduction of the forty-four-hour working week. It had begun with just twenty thousand workers from the engineering sector, but they were quickly joined by every major workplace in Belfast. Electricity and gas were switched off while essential government services were brought to a halt in actions tantamount to a complete shutdown of the city. In a stunning show of workers' unity, the mainly Protestant engineering workforce was led by a Catholic, Charles McKay. For a period it appeared as if the committee leading the strike was in control of the city. The lord mayor of Belfast declared that municipal authorities were "entirely at the mercy of the strike committee."[7] As in 1907, journalists sensed the rumblings of revolutionary upheaval: "Soviet has an unpleasant sound in English ears, and one uses it with hesitation; but it nevertheless appears to be the fact that the Strike Committee have taken upon themselves, with the involuntary acquiescence of the civic authority, some of the attributes of an industrial soviet."[8]

Despite the fact that both of these strikes went down to defeat, they played an important role in shaping the contours of politics throughout the home rule crisis. Orangeism was not just crucial to the Unionist elites as a means to unite Protestants against an independent Ireland; it was also a method of protecting their class interests by weakening trade unionism and dividing the working class. As the historian John Gray puts it, "For Belfast's employers, economic interest and the politics of Unionism were inextricably linked, and they accordingly saw in any major economic agitation—something serious enough in itself—a more fundamentally destabilising threat."[9] However, despite the significance of the labor revolts of 1907 and 1919, the working class in Belfast never became a force conscious of its own power to shape events, and it was left without effective political representation throughout the constitutional crisis. The "Workers' Republic" espoused by socialists like James Connolly, which alone stood a chance of winning support across the sectarian divide, was not championed by any significant force in the country, and as a result workers in the North remained divided behind middle class–led nationalist and Unionist blocs.

Important too was the impact of the defeat of the labor movement, which left its leading activists dejected and demoralized, and opened the door for other forces to intervene and shape the period in their own class interests. Britain took advantage of this impasse to impose a partitioned Ireland—based on the two parliaments announced in 1919 and solidified by the formation of the Northern Ireland state in 1921. This was not the inevitable result of some innate and irreconcilable cultural difference between Protestants and Catholics (or "two nations" in academic parlance), as the history of both the 1907 and 1919 labor unrest attests. Rather, the carve-up of Ireland into two partitioned states was the distillation of a prolonged social crisis involving different class actors, whose ultimate resolution showed the distinct etch marks of an imperial carve-up. As historian Fergal McCluskey observes:

> The British political elite supported Ulster unionists in order to subvert home rule and, failing that, handicap any independent state to the extent that it remained a virtual British possession. . . . The partition of Ireland did not rely on the existence of two nations or on fears of religious persecution, but rather on the determination of a Tory political elite, which included the Ulster unionist leaders, to preserve imperial interests.[10]

Connolly had warned that such a scenario would be disastrous for the labor movement and would lead to a "carnival of reaction" on both sides of the new border:

> Let us remember that the Orange aristocracy now fighting for its supremacy in Ireland has at all times been based upon a denial of the common human rights of the Irish people; that the Orange Order was not founded to safeguard religious freedom, but to deny religious freedom, and that it raised this religious question, not for the sake of any religion, but in order to use religious zeal in the interests of the oppressive property rights of rack-renting landlords and sweating capitalists. . . . Such a scheme as that agreed to by Redmond and Devlin, the betrayal of the national democracy of industrial Ulster would mean a carnival of reaction both North and South, would set back the wheels of progress, would destroy the oncoming unity of the Irish Labour movement and paralyse all advanced movements whilst it endured.
> To it Labour should give the bitterest opposition, against it Labour in Ulster should fight even to the death, if necessary, as our fathers fought before us.[11]

This warning, unheeded by both the labor movement and the republican leadership, quickly proved prophetic. Unionist elites were intent on copper-fastening their control by smashing any resistance to the new state. Through relentless sectarian agitation Unionists and their supporters whipped up tensions throughout the North. Loy-alist paramilitaries enacted a policy of murderous reprisals against Northern Catholic civilians for attacks carried out against British forces elsewhere in Ireland. Attacks by republicans on the police in Belfast became the pretext for unleashing a wave of state repression and sectarian violence, culminating in loyalist-led pogroms that saw thousands expelled from their homes and thousands more out of their workplaces. Anyone considered subversive was a target. In the main this meant the minority Catholic community. But the violence also targeted those Protestant socialists and trade unionists who re-fused to lend support to the pogrom and were therefore regarded by loyalism as "traitors." A Catholic worker who in July 1920 witnessed the violence accompanying the formation of the Northern state de-scribed the scene in the shipyards:

> The gates were smashed down with sledges, the vests and shirts of those at work were torn open to see if the men were wearing any Catholic emblems, and woe betide the man who was. One man was set upon, thrown into the dock, had to swim the Musgrave Channel, and having been pelted with rivets, had to swim two or three miles, to emerge in streams of blood and rush to the police office in a nude state.[12]

In the violence that followed the shipyard expulsions, twenty-eight people were killed and 1,766 wounded. Overall, between 1920 and 1922, 8,750 people were expelled from their jobs and 23,000 driven out of their homes.[13] The vast majority of the victims of this violence were Catholics. But Protestants were affected too, especially "rotten prods"—as they were labeled by loyalists—who had a history of workplace militancy or links with socialist groups. At least one out of every four workers expelled was Protestant.[14]

The impact on the labor movement in Northern Ireland was devastating. With the exception of the Amalgamated Society of Joiners and Carpenters, not a single union acted in defense of the Catholic workers expelled from their jobs. Under the pressure of events the British Trades Union Congress sent a delegation to Bel-fast to investigate, but no action was taken. Those who lost their jobs were never reinstated, and no union demanded that they should be. In evading their responsibility to uphold the rights of their Catholic members, the trade unions rendered themselves impotent in resisting the further division of the labor movement. Following the expulsions, a huge Union Jack was unfurled at the shipyards. Unionist leader James Craig was invited to open the shameful proceedings.[15] "Do I approve of the actions you boys have taken in the past?" he asked, in relation to the recent violence. "I say yes!"[16]

The impetus for the violence had clearly come from above. The newly formed B-Specials—one of several auxiliary police forces, with its ranks recruited directly out of the loyalist Ulster Volunteer Force—were at the heart of the sectarian attacks. Parallel to the state's role, sectarian organizations grew at the base of society, among the Protestant working class. The Ulster Protestant Association (UPA)—a paramilitary group made up of working-class men described by an RUC district inspector as having the sole aim of "extermination of Catholics by any means"—orchestrated much of the violence.[17] The rise of the UPA, and of extreme loyalism more generally during this period, can only be understood in class terms. While the expulsions from the shipyards were in many ways the very antithesis of the class unity of 1907 or 1919, they shared, paradoxically, the same underlying motivations. The sectarianism of the 1920s was, like the labor unrest of previous decades, driven by economic degradation. In 1920 the economy in the North of Ireland nosedived, leaving thousands out of work and ushering in an employer-led offensive on wages and conditions. The labor movement's ability to channel this discontent in a class direction, however, was severely hampered by its refusal over many years to directly challenge sectarianism. In the absence of a robust labor response to the economic crisis that might have undercut sectarian agitation, "forces emerged," according to one historian of the period, with a "simple alternative to the trade unions—to provide more jobs remove Catholics from the workplaces."[18]

It was a combustible mix. Egged on by Unionist Party politicians, the UPA and other forces used the prevailing economic degradation in the city as a stick to beat Catholic workers who, they claimed, had "stolen Protestant jobs." In addition, they targeted Protestant labor militants, calling for the expulsion of "all Roman Catholics, Sinn Féiners, and Nationalists," as well as "all unreliable Protestants and socialists."[19] Local employers both helped to instigate this sectarianism and actively facilitated its resurgence. For example, employers gave permission for sectarian meetings to be held during working hours on the grounds of the shipyards at a time when all other political activity was prohibited. Local Unionist elites even formed their own Protestant labor organization, the Ulster Unionist Labour Association (UULA), in an attempt to corral working-class Protestants behind its banner and dissuade them from entering into the ranks of more left-wing or labor-oriented groups. The group's laborist credentials were, however, suspect to say the least: the UULA opposed the 1919 General Strike and according to one historian "in general . . . avoided any stance likely to be controversial or divisive to the wider Unionist movement."[20]

The state of Northern Ireland, in the words of one London-based conservative newspaper, was born out of "five weeks of ruthless persecution by boycott, fire, plunder and assault."[21] For its own selfish reasons the Unionist government was content to facilitate the rampage against Catholics. "For all the bourgeois respectability of the Unionist leadership," one historian noted, "their commitment to the rule of law was partial and conditional."[22] Thus the attitude of Unionist elites to violence was a pragmatic one: riots, workplace expulsions, and even murder were essential in establishing the new state, but in the long run the chaos and unpredictability was harmful to the economic prospects of the province. The unrestrained violence of this period could not be allowed to go on indefinitely, and as the government began to consolidate its position the street violence led by the UPA was sidelined in favor of more conventional means of social control.

To achieve this, Unionists set about constructing a formidable repressive apparatus that would harness the undisciplined sectarianism of the street and place it under state control. Two quasi-paramilitary groups, the B-Specials and the A-Specials, were formed, with around twenty-five thousand armed men between them. In addition, the militarized RUC police force was organized and armed with twenty-six thousand British Army rifles, to be backed up when necessary by sixteen battalions of British troops stationed across the six-county state.[23] Sir Charles Wickham, the inspector general of the RUC, stated in November 1921 that the formation of the Specials was a way of stemming "the growth of unauthorised loyalist defence forces," such as the UPA, and "obtaining the services of the best elements of these organizations" in the protection of the state.[24] This approach was accurately described in the House of Commons by Nationalist MP Joe Devlin as "[arming] pogromists to murder the Catholics." "Instead of paving stones and sticks," he observed, "they are to be given rifles."[25] These organizations were almost exclusively Protestant and militantly sectarian to their core. At a cabinet meeting on May 31, 1922, Prime Minister Lloyd George claimed that Mussolini's Fascisti provided an "exact analogy" for the B-Specials, which the British government had organized and armed.[26] George Gilmore, a republican writer and activist, later claimed that "when Sir Oswald Mosley, the leader of Fascism in England, visited Belfast with the object of extending his organization to Northern Ireland, Lord Craigavon assured him that it was unnecessary—that Northern Ireland had already, in its armed special constabulary, a Fascist force in being."[27]

The new state deployed a raft of repressive legislation. In particular, the Special Powers Act (1922) placed considerable power in the hands of the state, allowing for arrest, search, detention without warrant, the death penalty for arms-related offenses, and the banning of processions and marches deemed to be a threat to the state. In effect, it allowed for the complete suspension of civil liberties at the drop of a hat. Later, the apartheid-era South African prime minister Hendrik Verwoerd said he "would be willing to exchange all the legislation of this sort for one clause of the Northern Ireland Special Powers Act."[28] While some of the apparatus would be scaled back in years to come (the A-Specials were abolished in 1925), the repressive machinery remained largely intact—effectively rendering Northern Ireland a paramilitary state from its outset.

The Unionist Party government, however, could not rely on military might alone: from early on it was clear that they would have to use a combination of consent and coercion to stabilize the new state. Having survived the constitutional challenge posed by Irish nationalism, the state still faced potential opposition. To begin with, they had to contend with the minority Catholic population who, having been violently suppressed in the preceding years, were wary of, if not openly hostile to, its existence. Catholics made up perhaps a third of the population—not enough to present a challenge to the Unionist status quo but more than sufficient numbers to fuel sectarian paranoia among the governing elites. In the minds of the Unionist ruling class, Catholics were vermin who, if left to their own devices, would eventually outbreed the Protestant majority and overrun the state. These views were held by many, including Northern Ireland's first prime minister, Lord Craigavon. In a meeting with the Australian prime minister Joseph Lyons, Craigavon displayed his virulent anti-Catholicism, recounted here by the wife of Lyons:

> Lord Craigavon, the fiercely anti-Catholic prime minister of Northern Ireland, asked Joe at a banquet: "Lyons, have you got many Catholics in Australia?" "Oh, about one in five," Joe had replied. "Well watch them, Lyons, watch them," Craigavon had urged. "They breed like bloody rabbits."[29]

Unionist fear of the minority Catholic population was coupled with a mistrust of the local labor movement and aggravated by the spread of Bolshevism and the postwar revolutionary upheaval shaking Europe. This paranoia on the part of Ulster's elites was not altogether irrational. Much of Europe in this period was gripped by working-class unrest and political upheaval in the aftermath of the 1917 Russian Revolution—in Hungary and the German province of Bavaria short-lived, soviet republics had been formed, while left-led uprisings had occurred in Berlin and Vienna. Even in those countries that saw no specific revolution, such as Italy or Britain, incessant industrial unrest and huge general strikes would have a major impact on politics for some time. No doubt the ruling class in Ulster kept a keen eye on these unfolding events.

While the threat posed by global workers' movements had been temporarily checked by 1921, the spectre of its revival continued to haunt the bourgeoisie in the North. In effect, the state saw the main threat to its stability as emanating from either nationalist unrest or labor militancy. In order to stave off these threats the Unionist government sought to kill two birds with one stone through a strategy of sectarian populism and the creation of the "Orange State." The state would be based on a combination of discrimination and exclusion against Catholics and a sectarian populism aimed at winning the allegiance of Protestant workers to unionism through preference in the allocation of jobs, services, and housing. Consolidation of the Orange State therefore had the twin consequences of subduing the nationalist population through repression while in the process neutralizing the local labor movement by splitting it down the middle. This allowed the ruling class to stabilize its political control through the Unionist Party and create an environment favorable to elite power.

The first part of this strategy was to institute a systematic program of exclusion aimed at the Catholic population. In order to achieve this, Unionists effectively rigged the electoral system to ensure their domination. Electoral boundaries were redrawn to create artificial Unionist majorities—in 1920, twenty-five local councils in the six counties were in Nationalist hands, but by 1924, they retained only two. This gerrymandering was most flagrant in Derry, where despite being home to a Catholic majority, Unionists maintained a grip on the council for the next half century. The Northern Ireland Parliament itself was a stale institution, where the inbuilt Unionist majority rendered even the limited normal processes of democracy null and void. Moreover, the effects of gerrymandering were permanent: no Unionist-controlled council has ever been retaken by Nationalists, and the local parliament would be controlled by a single party for its entire existence.

While Catholics were certainly oppressed by the new structures of the Northern Ireland state, the traditional national leadership mounted no serious or active opposition. Rather than embark upon a serious and sustained campaign of resistance to partition, the nationalist middle class acquiesced, preferring instead to carve out a space for itself within the new arrangements. The Catholic Church would control schooling within nationalist areas, and politicians like Joe Devlin would stake out a position for themselves as communal representatives of the minority population. Rather than act as a harbinger for future resentment against unionism, therefore, this Catholic state-within-a-state, according to one historian, "acted as a check against any radical attempt to challenge the status quo."[30]

Despite the weakness of official Nationalist opposition to the state, sectarian division proved crucial in preserving Unionist dominance. To maintain this state of affairs, unionism had to offer something to its working-class supporters. In return for their loyalty to the state, Protestant workers were favored in the allocation of housing and jobs. Control of local government gave the Unionist Party the ability to allocate employment and housing along sectarian lines. Discrimination wasn't confined to the state, but its enforcement there gave it legitimacy in the private sector. The exclusion of Catholics from major industries in the North during the pogroms was further entrenched, with private-sector exclusion aggressively enforced after the formation of the state.[31] While at times of economic growth or exceptional labor demand (as during the Second World War) Catholics might secure employment in the lower echelons of the unskilled workforce, they could also expect to be the first to be laid off when the situation worsened.

These arrangements had a powerful effect in shaping the local labor movement. In the absence of any class-based alternative it seemed to many Protestant workers that they were better off supporting the Unionists rather than throwing in their lot with their Catholic fellow workers. But all was not as it seemed. While Protestant workers generally enjoyed higher living standards than Catholics, the divisions in the labor movement allowed local employers to attack living standards across the board. The pogroms of the 1920s had drastically undermined the capacity of the trade union movement to build a broad, class-based movement that might win concessions for all workers. The employers used this weakness to their advantage, and, in the aftermath of the pogroms, wages and conditions for the majority of workers "plunged downward."[32] By 1925 shipyard workers could expect just forty-seven shillings for a forty-seven-hour week (in 2015 currency, this would be around £250 a week)—far below the earlier standard of eighty-seven shillings—and wages for the majority of Belfast's shipyard laborers were far lower than their counterparts in Britain.[33] Housing conditions overall were much worse than in Britain, and unemployment in Northern Ireland was typically double the rate across the water. In 1924 the Unionist government spent just £4 per head on social services, compared with £14 in Britain.[34] So while Protestant workers could expect more than Catholics, their "privilege" was in many ways an illusion: Protestants gained a sense of entitlement and empowerment over their Catholic counterparts but little in the way of real material advancement. The reality was that while Catholics bore the main brunt of elite rule in the Orange State, Protestant workers lost out too, as the ruling class exploited labor's weaknesses to drive down wages and living standards for workers across the North.

The Northern Ireland state garnered a degree of stability as the 1920s went on. The threat from Irish nationalism faded as the new Southern ruling class set about consolidating its own position, leaving Northern nationalists and republicans divided and demoralized. The labor movement recovered to a degree but did not come anywhere near reclaiming the heights of militancy seen in 1919. The Orange State stabilized, and "by 1923," according to one commentator, "unionist dominance was incontestable."[35] In 1924 the Northern Ireland government was granted a coat of arms by royal warrant: its symbol, a red hand with a crown above it, was an unwittingly apt one for a state created to preserve the power of the privileged by people with blood on their hands.

Chapter 2

UNEMPLOYMENT AND RELIEF IN THE NORTH OF IRELAND

U nemployment has always been a problem in any advanced capitalist society. In the North of Ireland, however, this problem
was aggravated by the cruel and unfair system that governed
those out of work. The system, known as the Poor Laws, was import-
ed from Britain and is probably best remembered as the subject of
Charles Dickens's second novel, *Oliver Twist*, about an orphan boy
born into a life of poverty and misfortune in a workhouse in an un-
identified town in industrial Britain. An early example of realist fic-
tion, Dickens's work exposed conditions faced by tens of thousands
of people housed in the hated workhouses, and drew attention to the
inhumane conditions provided under the Poor Laws. Under mounting criticism, the main tenets of this system had by the 1930s been
abolished across Britain and Ireland in all but one place: Northern
Ireland. Almost a hundred years after the publication of Dickens's
novel, Belfast's large unemployed population remained subject to
many of the same horrendous conditions he had exposed so forcefully all those years ago.

The Poor Laws were an institutionalized form of class control.
Their origins can be traced back to nineteenth-century Britain. Fearing that the widespread destitution then gripping the countryside
might fuel the spread of rural agitation, the British government en-
deavoured to find a solution to the wandering masses of unemployed
it regarded as a threat to social stability. In 1833, Prime Minister Earl

Grey set up a commission to examine the working of the Poor Law system in Britain. Ostensibly set up to deal with poverty, the review was no philanthropic undertaking; instead, those who oversaw the commission were, according to one historian, "strongly influenced by the notion that most of the destitute were lazy or idle and could provide for themselves if they tried hard enough."[1]

In 1834 the commission's report was published: in it they recommended that a system of workhouses be created across the country in order to house and offer "relief" to the poor. Local ratepayers would pay for the construction and maintenance of the workhouses, and would then elect a "board of guardians" to oversee their administration. In 1837 the British government introduced a bill to extend these Poor Laws to Ireland. The majority of MPs from Ireland opposed the bill, including the middle-class Nationalist MP Daniel O'Connell, who observed that "the work imposed under the Poor Law upon the idle population was only a kind of slave labour."[2] Despite this opposition, however, the Irish Poor Law Act was passed in 1838 and the country divided into 130 unions in which workhouses would be built. As in Britain, a board of guardians elected by ratepayers, drawn mainly from the property-owning middle and upper classes, would be tasked with running the workhouses.

The Irish Poor Laws combined an early and extremely limited form of social welfare with a harsh system of enforced labor. The workhouses were both feared and hated in equal measures, with many preferring to starve on the streets rather than submit themselves to its masochistic rigor. On entry, "paupers" were separated by age and sex. The "inmates" were unpaid, could claim very few rights, and enjoyed no organized labor representation. In return for shelter and basic food supplies, they were expected to work long hours performing gruelling, menial tasks and to live within cramped, confined, damp, and disease-ridden dorms. Their diet consisted of meager supplies of potatoes, buttermilk, and oatmeal. The very harshness of the workhouses was no mere accident—conditions were "conceived to deter all but the most desperate poor from seeking support."[3]

In 1842, while living and working in Manchester, Friedrich Engels compiled a study from his own observations of the conditions of working class life. In his classic account, Engels railed against the inhumane treatment of urban workers in England but poured particular scorn on the workhouses regulated under the Poor Laws. His harrowing description of such conditions in England is worth quoting at length:

> To make sure that Relief be applied for only in the most extreme cases and after every other effort had failed, the workhouse has been made the most repulsive residence which the refined ingenuity of a Malthusian can invent. The food is worse than that of the most ill-paid working-man while employed, and the work harder, or they might prefer the workhouse to their wretched existence outside. . . . To prevent the "superfluous" from multiplying, and "demoralised" parents from influencing their children, families are broken up; the husband is placed in one wing, the wife in another, the children in a third, and they are permitted to see one another only at stated times after long intervals, and then only when they have, in the opinion of the officials, behaved well. . . . As in life, so in death. The poor are dumped into the earth like infected cattle. . . . Can any one wonder that the poor decline to accept public Relief under these conditions? That they starve rather than enter these bastilles?[4]

The conditions inside Belfast workhouses under the Irish Poor Laws were no less harsh than those Engels had described in Manchester. One significant difference was that the Poor Laws in Britain allowed for a form of Outdoor Relief in exceptional circumstances—whereby assistance would be afforded to the poor in the form of money or food, without the requirement to enter the workhouse—a measure rejected by authorities in Ireland. The mass starvation during the Great Hunger of the 1840s—or an t-Ocras Mór as it was known to Ireland's then largely Gaelic-speaking population—changed this. Numbers of those seeking admission to the workhouses—accessing what was called Indoor Relief—swelled due to the widespread destitution of the time, putting considerable strain on the system. In an effort to relieve the pressure, the 1847 Poor Law Relief Extension Act was passed, allowing for the administration of Outdoor Relief to people outside of the workhouse. "The precedent of outdoor relief,

once accepted, proved impossible to abandon," according to one historian of the period, and this temporary provision was extended in
the Local Government of Ireland Act (1898), allowing local guardians to provide Outdoor Relief in periods of exceptional distress.[5]

Although the unemployed now enjoyed a legal right to Outdoor
Relief, its actual distribution was left to the discretion of the local
boards of guardians, who subjected workers to a strict and degrading qualification process. Those seeking ODR had to exhaust all of
their savings and then attend an often humiliating interview with
the local guardians to prove that they were not work-shy. The Belfast Board of Guardians proved notoriously tightfisted in dispensing
relief outside of the workhouses. In 1906, for example, there were
only 8,732 people receiving Outdoor Relief across Ulster, compared
with 11,066 in the workhouses. But the situation in Belfast was
much worse: in the entire city just eighty-seven people were granted Outdoor Relief while 3,819 were confined in the workhouse.[6]
The Guardians loathed granting money to people they viewed as
lazy and work-shy, exhibiting a distinct class prejudice. They regarded their mission as one of punishment rather than relief. As Maurice Goldring puts it, the Guardians were "drawn from the mainly
lower middle class" and were "strongly Calvinistic." "They felt en-
dowed with a mission: destitute or unemployed paupers were being
punished by God for some sin they had committed, and they, the
Guardians, were part of the Wrath of God."[7]

When the Northern Ireland state was formed after partition,
the Poor Law system remained intact. While the Southern state had
abolished the Poor Law in 1924 and the British state followed suit
a few years later, the hated workhouses were still in operation across
Belfast. Henry Miller, an officer of the Belfast Union, noted in 1942
that there had been "little change in the method of providing Indoor
Relief (in the workhouse) in Northern Ireland; the system adopted
by the Poor Law Relief Act remains very much the same to-day. The
accommodation for inmates has been little changed in a hundred
years."[8] By the summer of 1925 the Northern government had introduced tight restrictions as to who would receive unemployment
benefits. Under the new regulations, workers were eligible only if

they had been working and paying employment insurance for two years and if they passed a stringent means test proving they were genuinely seeking work. The outcome of these requirements was obvious: in a country with such high levels of unemployment, large sections of the populace had not seen work for two years and were thus denied benefits.

In addition to cutting the relief rolls, the Belfast Guardians worked consistently to reduce the level of relief paid. The Guardians viewed themselves not as representatives of the poor but of the middle and upper classes—the ratepayers who had elected them. In 1927 they decided to cut Outdoor Relief to anyone who had been receiving it for more than twelve months, demanding that the government introduce a labor test to prove that those on ODR were not work-shy. In effect this meant that relief recipients would be forced to work for free to receive their measly benefits. The government agreed to the proposal, and in February 1928 the first task work schemes began—laying pavement for Belfast Corporation Housing. In 1927, some 6,446 people were given relief in Belfast. By their aggressive efforts the Guardians had reduced this figure to less than a thousand just a year later.[9]

Another significant element set the Poor Laws in Northern Ireland apart from welfare systems elsewhere: sectarianism. While the high level of unemployment was often a source of unrest in Northern Ireland, it was also a powerful means of control. The existence of a sizeable unemployed population—what Engels had termed a "reserve army of labor"—acted to dampen workplace activism among workers who feared that they could be replaced at any moment by the eager throngs of the unemployed waiting outside the factory gates. The Unionists used their control of the boards of guardians to further entrench this fear. The interview process was perhaps the worst part. Every Tuesday at noon, the Belfast Board of Guardians met in the Belfast Union to assess would-be applicants. Upon entering, applicants were met by the board members, who sat in line beneath a large Union Jack, in an atmosphere of calculated intimidation and snobbery. Paddy Devlin records that applicants had no legal representation with them and were quizzed by the overwhelmingly male board: "No subject was sacred, no question, no matter how personal, was ruled out. Detailed information was asked for on the applicants' private life and discussed cynically by the Board. Often Catholics were told to ignore Church teachings on sex."[10]

For Unionist elites, the administration of relief was an important political tool, and the boards would often give preference to those they viewed as loyal. The effect was that many chose to keep their mouths shut and toe the line lest they fall foul of employers or the board: militant trade union activity could result not only in the loss of one's job but also the loss of any source of income for the applicant's family.[11]

The sectarianism inherent in the Poor Laws drew some criticism from the Catholic middle classes: West Belfast MP Joe Devlin often criticized its operation in the House of Commons. While Devlin was compelled to take up the issue of Poor Laws in order to serve his constituents and maintain his electoral seat, the opposition from the Catholic middle classes was often weak and rhetorical. For example, they refrained from joining the chorus demanding an increase in the rate paid to the unemployed. The *Irish News*—the newspaper of the Catholic middle class—criticized the running of the relief scheme but was more concerned about the stress it was putting on ratepayers. The paper said that putting more men to work on ODR schemes was "urgently necessary" and would "have the merit of effecting a considerable saving in the city rates"; editors called on people to imagine the "valuable work that could be performed within the city boundaries" and relished the idea of compelling the poor to pave the city's streets and improve its general appearance without compensation.[12]

Although a principled opposition to the Poor Laws was not to be found within either unionism or nationalism, a more robust protest did emerge from other quarters in the early days of the Northern state. Unemployment was always relatively high in Northern Ireland, but the precarious state of the economy would occasionally lead to a dramatic rise, unleashing strife and agitation. By the beginning of 1922 nearly sixty-eight thousand, or 25 percent, of the state's insured population were unemployed.[13] At the end of 1922, an unemployed delegation organized regular meetings at Custom

House Square in the center of Belfast to highlight their treatment at the hands of the government; rallies involved members of both the NILP and the Unemployed Workers Committee. The movement saw steady growth throughout 1922, but numbers at rallies rarely surpassed five hundred, and the campaign began to decline, receding as the economy began to recover and unemployment gradually dipped.[14] It would, however, be only a temporary reprieve.

In 1925 the Northern Ireland economy again went into recession, causing a more substantial outbreak of protest over unemployment. In September there were fifty-six thousand people unemployed in the North, rising two months later by more than eight thousand, leaving 24 percent of the workforce jobless (compared with 11 percent unemployment in Britain).[15] Growing frustration was at first expressed not on the street but at the ballot box: owing to their firm stance on unemployment and the Poor Laws, three Labour MPs were elected in Northern Ireland. Emboldened by Labour's breakthrough and with thousands facing starvation, an Unemployed Workers Committee was formed, and a trade union–led campaign was launched. In Parliament, one Labour MP warned the government about their treatment of the unemployed:

> I warn the government very seriously that they have a very direct and definite responsibility. If they are not prepared to accept that responsibility and do something for the large number of people unemployed at the present time—the large number of people who are starving and whose wives and families are starving through no fault of their own—then there will be a day of reckoning as far as the government is concerned . . . and in a way they will not like.[16]

This warning to the government was more than empty words, and important forces within the labor movement called a mass demonstration: the Unemployed Workers Committee, the NILP, and the Belfast Trades Council (a body that drew together local trade unions in the city, then led by figures sympathetic to the NILP) called for a mass rally to take place on October 6, when the Northern Ireland Parliament opened for business. The rally would assemble at Belfast City Hall and march to Parliament, then housed in buildings on Botanic Avenue. To build for the protest, organizers held local meetings across Belfast, at which a militant mood was evident. At one meeting in Belfast in September 1925, Independent Labour Party member Hugh Gemmell threatened to make Prime Minister James Craig's knees knock "like bones in a jazz band," while another speaker said that "the revolution was coming."[17]

It was clear from the response across the city that the planned unemployment protest would be massive. However, the Unionist government had one ploy left to use against the movement: the Special Powers Act. Just days before the rally, the minister for Home Affairs, Dawson Bates, banned the rally and arranged for a massive mobilization of state forces to be on hand in case the march went ahead. Unfortunately, for all their talk that the "revolution was coming," the trade union leaders and the Labour politicians called off the march. The demoralization generated by this retreat among the ordinary unemployed would have disastrous consequences for the movement, marking the end of any mass agitation around the issue in the 1920s.

The return of the unemployment question to politics in Northern Ireland originated not in Ulster but at the center of global finance capital thousands of miles away. On October 24, 1929, the bell tolled in the New York Stock Exchange on Wall Street, signalling the beginning of daily trading. What followed sent shock waves across the world: the market lost 11 percent of its value instantly and the stocks on the exchange had fallen by almost a third by the end of the day. In the weeks that followed contagion spread across markets into every part of the world, wiping out the wealth of thousands of finance capitalists in an instant and destroying the savings of millions of ordinary people in the process. The day that would become known as "Black Thursday" carried with it ominous consequences for the rest of the world.

The crash caught capitalists and bourgeois economists completely unaware. Global capitalism had experienced a period of sustained growth throughout the 1920s, and establishment commentators assumed the boom would last indefinitely. The American economist Irving Fisher stated on the eve of the crash that stock prices had reached "what looks like a permanently high plateau," while his British counterpart John Maynard Keynes famously assured his students that "there will be no further crash in our lifetime."[18] The "Roaring Twenties," as they were known, were the result of the massive expansion of the United States as a global economic power. US growth acted as an impetus for a boom in other countries: in Germany massive loans from the United States fed a recovery from deep postwar economic crisis while countries like Britain prospered from increasing global trade. On the markets finance capitalists made millions in a trading culture defined by rampant speculation. But the signs that all was not well had been there—in the days and weeks leading up to the crash, the markets had experienced considerable turbulence, with prices rising and falling in periods of high volume trading.[19] At the time, this volatility was considered a blip on the radar.

The economic growth of the 1920s was built on shaky ground, and, as the US economy began to slow in 1929, speculation and lending increased dramatically. It was an unsustainable state of affairs. On Black Thursday these problems came to a head, and the US economy went into a nosedive. A year into the Depression its industrial output was lower than its pre-1914 levels. By 1932, five thousand local banks had failed in the United States and one in three workers was unemployed. With the epicenter of global capitalism in decline, the rest of the world followed suit. The value of world trade collapsed to a third of the 1929 figure, and unemployment rose rapidly. In Germany, which relied heavily on US loans, the effects were disastrous, with some six million workers made redundant.

Industrial employers in Belfast had been keeping a close eye on events unfolding across the Atlantic. The day after Black Thursday, the financial section of the Unionist-affiliated *Belfast Newsletter* commented on the "unprecedented excitement" in the markets after the "New York Stocks avalanche" but saw no reason to worry, reporting that "no changes on the local boards" had occurred at stock exchanges in Belfast.[20] It was not until four days after the crash that news of the "Wall Street Panic" hit its main headlines: on October 30 the *Newsletter*'s lead article was entitled "Pandemonium and Panic—the chaos spreads."[21] The local media in Belfast remained confident that market recovery would be swift. On October 31 the *Belfast Telegraph* reported that "the worst is now over. . . . It is generally felt that Wall Street has weathered the worst storm in its history with commendable stability, and that the complete lack of failures is striking proof of the soundness of its financial organisation."[22]

As the predicted stabilization of the markets failed to materialize, the capitalist class in Northern Ireland grew increasingly alarmed. One paper described those who were pessimistic about economic prospects as "croakers"—warning that gloomy talk could only do damage to the local economy.[23] In the months that followed, the local press continued to talk in glowing terms about the prospects for local industry: reports on the linen and shipbuilding industries looked to prosperous days ahead. The *Newsletter* was especially quick to reject any notion that the Wall Street Crash could be blamed on the capitalist system: "A certain number of persons . . . state that the present system is 'all wrong.' . . . If those who object to the present system said that some parts of it are wrong [then] all sane persons . . . would agree[,] but when they declare that the present system is 'all wrong' they are talking through their hats."[24]

Unfortunately, wishful thinking and a head-in-the-sand approach could not alter the economic reality—Northern Ireland was heading into a deep recession. The Northern economy was especially vulnerable to a slump in the global market for three reasons. Firstly it was primarily an export-driven economy with a weak internal market and an overreliance on two or three key industries. This meant that a weakening of foreign markets would result in a decline in orders, ripping the center of the economy to pieces. This vulnerability was exacerbated in the North because the region was primarily an exporter of heavy industrial goods—orders for extremely expensive ships, for example, were unlikely to be placed in times of economic uncertainty.[25] Secondly, the Northern economy had been showing a steady decline for some years before the onset of the Depression. Its former position as a key manufacturer for the British Empire was steadily disappearing, as it faced increasing competition from emerging manufacturing centers elsewhere in the world. This new state of affairs contrasted sharply with Belfast's industrial heyday, when

Ulster enjoyed an effective monopoly in its exports. Lastly, while the global boom of the 1920s had spared the Northern economy from feeling the full effects of this declining position, the state had been beset with difficulties throughout the decade, and the local economy remained precarious. As historian Jonathan Bardon argues, throughout this period the Northern Ireland economy remained in a weak position: "The Roaring Twenties were experienced elsewhere [but] had no meaning to [local] citizens," meaning that the North entered a period of deep global economic crisis already in a vulnerable state.[26]

It is unlikely that the panic on the floors of Wall Street immediately registered in the mills, factories, and shipyards of Belfast some three thousand miles away. But in the anarchic world of global capitalism the choices made by a tiny number of people at the center of the system would have profound consequences for millions of ordinary people throughout the world. John Hyde, a shipyard worker in Belfast recalls that in 1930, "The clouds that had begun to show throughout the world really closed over the top of the Belfast shipyard."[27] The once-mighty Belfast shipping industry was in serious trouble. Orders placed in the 1920s kept the shipyards afloat temporarily, but disaster lay ahead. From 1930 onward, orders for new ships began to fall drastically. Between December 1931 and May 1934 not a single ship was launched from the shipyards. The effect on those who worked there was dramatic—the shipyard workforce fell from 10,428 in 1930 to just 1,554 in 1932.[28] At its height in the 1920s there had been twenty thousand men employed in the two main Belfast shipyards. Workman & Clark, founded in 1879 and one of the oldest shipbuilding companies in Belfast, struggled through the recession, finally failing and putting its entire workforce on the breadline. Thomas Carnduff, a Protestant shipyard worker and playwright, described the mood among the workforce as Workman & Clark closed its gates:

> And what a finish! Perhaps the weather was concerned in the plot. The rain fell in proverbial cat-and-dog fashion as we made our way along the quayside. It beat our faces, trickled off our caps down the backs of our necks, ran down our overcoats into our boots, leaving nothing dry but our throats. We lifted our time-boards at the gatehouse and hurried on. It was breaking dawn. A wet miserable

dawn. The devil's own way of heralding a catastrophe. I tripped over an angle bar in the dusk and floundered into a minute lake, splashing my comrades in a shower of mud. My mate cursed sourly and told me to watch my step. Another time he would have laughed heartily.

We halted a moment under cover to shake the raindrops off our caps. The panorama of what had recently been a shipyard lay before us. The long avenues of tall staging poles stood like sentinels. How the worker manages to hide his real feelings has always been a mystery to me—and I am one of them myself. An ominous silence was now creeping over the ship. Hammers had ceased to ring; caulking tools were silent. No hum of the drill. No life.... In a few moments, we had ceased to be employed workmen.... And there was no escape. The thing was wearing me down.[29]

Other industries fared just as badly or worse. Linen had once been the staple of the Northern Irish economy, transforming the region and drawing Belfast into the "age of the factory"; from a town of just 37,000 in 1821 Belfast had grown into a major industrial city of 387,000 by 1911, and much of that growth had been fueled by the dramatic rise of linen. Demand spiked during the First World War, largely due to military orders, but began to recede as the war came to an end. Global competition caused a reduction in market prices at the same time that changes in fashion reduced demand. The crash of 1929 was the most serious crisis the industry had ever faced, and would prove to be the beginning of a terminal decline. The linen factories were part of the fabric of life in Belfast, tied to the culture and the social structure of the city by a thousand threads. Northern Ireland's linen workforce represented a majority of linen workers in the United Kingdom, and a decline in the industry affected the region disproportionately. In 1924 the linen industry had employed 87,000 workers, but by five years into the Depression this had fallen by more than 25,000.[30]

Unemployment in Northern Ireland skyrocketed. In a region where the unemployment level had rarely fallen below 15 percent this would have a serious impact on working-class life. Across the board, trade unions reported a steep rise in the numbers out of work—the Sheet Metal Workers' Union reported half of its members out of work, while more than 40 percent in the building trades had lost their jobs.[31] By 1932 the official unemployment rate was 28 percent—or seventy-two thousand registered out of work—but the real figure was probably closer to one hundred thousand. In Belfast alone there were forty-eight thousand registered unemployed. For many workers the experience of unemployment was a shock. As a resident of Belfast at the time explained, "Short time unemployment was common enough. It simply meant a tightening of the belt for a while. If essential payments fell behind they could always be cleared off at so much weekly, once work was resumed: but this was something different. As months stretched into years, people began to despair."[32]

The intensifying economic depression would have important political consequences. The Unionist establishment's political power had always been predicated on its support within a section of the Protestant working class. During the 1920s Unionist politicians could plausibly claim that in return for their allegiance at the polls Protestant workers were rewarded through economic discrimination. Unionist politicians had been well aware of the dangers of deteriorating conditions for workers. In 1925, during a debate on the introduction of contributory pensions, James Craig, the first prime minister of Northern Ireland, warned his government that "the screws would be put on if we refuse to give the same benefits to people living in our own area" as in Britain.[33] There were others in the Unionist establishment, however, who held much more conventional bourgeois views on monetary policy, and these two factions would diverge on how best to stabilize their power during the economic crisis. One group, based around Prime Minister Craig, Minister of Labour J. M. Andrews, and Minister of Home Affairs Richard Dawson Bates, feared that if they moved too quickly they would risk the loss of Protestant working-class support and lay the basis for a potential unity between Protestant and Catholic workers. This wing of the government sought to secure the status quo through a continuation of sectarian populism and preference for Protestants. A second faction was grouped around Minister of Finance Hugh Pollock, Parliamentary Secretary to the

Minister of Finance John Milne-Barbour, and head of the Northern
Ireland Civil Service Sir Wilfred Spender. This grouping emphasized
the need to balance the books and keep government spending in
check even if it impacted the mass of Protestants.[34]

With the onset of the Depression it was the anti-populist wing
of unionism, around Pollock, Milne-Barbour, and Spender, that
would came to the fore.[35] With the economy in free fall there could
be no room for the kind of sectarian populism favored by Craig and
his allies: jobs, wages, and social services would all be cut back. Jobs
and houses could not be provided to one section of the population
when no jobs or houses were available to be dispensed at all. In the
1930s Northern Ireland was the poorest region of the United Kingdom: by every standard of measurement living standards in Northern Ireland were far below the British average, and by the end of the
1930s average income per head in the North was just £64.7 compared with the UK average of £111.[36] In this increasingly desperate
context it became more and more difficult for Unionist politicians
to claim they were on the side of Protestant workers. Anger and dis-
illusionment in working-class areas began to grow, and the Orange
all-class alliance would soon show signs of fracture.

Unionist elites had good cause for concern. Unemployment was
affecting Protestant and Catholics equally, sharpening a cross-community sense of grievance. Life for those without work was harsh: poverty, malnutrition, and hunger were all to be found in the streets and
slums of Belfast. Housing was almost exclusively rented, and landlords
frequently resorted to confiscating the belongings of tenants unable
to pay their rent. Many poor people sold what furniture they owned
when times got hard. What furniture they had also tended to be rented, and local "tick men" would regularly come round door-to-door to
collect payments. Furniture was often taken from those unable to keep
up. Homes tended to be very cramped and stuffy, with windows rarely opened. The biggest killer in Belfast was pneumonia, followed by
tuberculosis (or consumption), and then influenza. In these years, the
basic diet for many working-class people deteriorated as well: meat
became a rarity for many, though cheaper cuts would be bought to use
in large pots of soup, which were made to last for two or three days.

While these conditions did not lead immediately to mass agitation, upheaval was only around the corner. Across the world unemployed movements began to emerge, often inspired by Communist agitation, threatening the local status quo and providing direction for the deep well of anger and desperation then taking hold.[37] On July 19, 1932, an *Irish News* editorial reported on a mass rally of military veterans in Washington, DC, seeking an early payment of their pensions due to high rates of unemployment. In describing events thought peculiar to the United States, the editors could have had no idea that similar scenes would be repeated in Belfast in a matter of weeks:

> The unemployment outlook in America grows everyday more serious . . . the 20,000 "bonus veterans" encamped at Washington [are] a living symbol and a public menace. Clothed in rags, leading an unutterable existence[,] this army of misery refuses to go home[.] Daily they become more demonstrative and threatening[.] The government is at its wit's end to know how to deal with the situation . . . it threatens martial law and the use of force but refrains . . . its indecisiveness may well be found in the fact that it fears that the forces of authority would prove a torch setting the American continent ablaze from end to end with the flames of revolutionary disorder bred in the inevitable discontent that widespread distress engenders.[38]

Northern Ireland's rulers, so accustomed to having things their own way, could not have failed to take note of the spread of unemployment agitation across the world. The roots of sectarianism were deep and had paralyzed the workers' movement in the North since the inception of the state. The threat of state repression was strong. But the sheer depths of the economic crisis were driving working-class people in both communities to seriously consider their options. The question of the hour had been raised forcefully by John Steinbeck in his gripping Depression-era novel, *The Grapes of Wrath*: "How can you frighten a man whose hunger is not only in his own cramped stomach but in the wretched bellies of his children? You can't scare him—he has known a fear beyond every other."[39]

Chapter 3

THE UNEMPLOYED GET ORGANIZED

I n 1932 the Northern Ireland economy was in free fall, and the region's unemployment figures continued to rise sharply. By late summer there were some seventy-two thousand registered and around thirty thousand unregistered unemployed. The official rate of unemployment stood at 28 percent, but in reality it was approaching the 40 percent mark.[1] For the many thousands of people who found themselves out of work—many for the first time in their adult lives—the grim reality of unemployment was a tremendous burden to bear, particularly for those who had a family to feed as well as themselves. The options facing the unemployed were extremely limited: they could seek new employment, of course, but no matter how hard they searched or what skills they could offer, most workers learned quickly that there were no jobs to be had. The more fortunate among the laboring classes could fall back on the unemployment insurance they had accumulated while working, but even this proved a temporary reprieve, lasting only 156 days until the money began to dry up.

As weeks turned into months and the months into years, fewer and fewer workers had any unemployment insurance left to draw upon. After the insurance payments ended an unemployed worker could apply for a transitional benefit, but to attain this you had to pass a strict means test, administered by the Board of Guardians, and thousands of unemployed people were not granted this benefit. All of these measures and loopholes meant that thousands of unemployed had no access to benefits at all. Their options, therefore, were Indoor Relief in the workhouse (which few choose), or Outdoor

43

Relief and the task work schemes. However, the Guardians did not plan enough schemes to accommodate all applicants and paid very little in relief, leaving thousands of people in dire straits. No benefit was available to people under eighteen, to married women, or to those who lived in a house where another person was working. The situation was starkest in Belfast where fifty thousand people found themselves unemployed, nearly half of them without access to any form of unemployment benefit.[2]

The region's Poor Law system was woefully unfit for the scale of the unemployment crisis. Belfast's workhouses could not possibly cope with the swelling numbers of unemployed, and the result of this was a steep growth in demand for Outdoor Relief. From the onset of economic crisis, the Board of Guardians had worked hard to keep as many people off relief as possible, using all manner of bureaucratic maneuvers in the process. Their intransigence was the product of neither pure folly nor the maverick actions of a local governing body, but rather the logical outcome of an austerity agenda set at the heart of the Unionist government. By and large representative of the wealthiest section of society, the government considered itself a caretaker for whatever capital remained in Northern Ireland. In particular, they sought to keep state spending as low as possible and were keen to avoid state-funded initiatives aimed at helping the unemployed, which could only be paid by a tax on the upper classes. In the Belfast Board of Guardians, the Unionist government found a willing accomplice: they continued to see their role as one of protecting the public purse while goading the poor back to work. The Guardians kept the rates of relief at abominably low levels, far lower than the equivalent in Britain: twelve shillings for a family of three in Belfast compared with twenty-three shillings in Liverpool, twenty-five shillings in Glasgow, or twenty-seven shillings in Northampton, for example.[3] The sheer scale of the crisis, however, forced them to allow more people onto relief lest they lose all public credibility. In January 1932 they granted Outdoor Relief in 884 cases affecting 4,008 people, and by September this had risen to 2,612, affecting nearly 12,000 people. Despite this increase in the provision of relief, its distribution remained restrictive and wholly inadequate, leaving thousands hungry and without any income at all.[4]

The unemployment crisis was having a devastating impact on Belfast. In 1932, the city was a sorry sight to see: its streets awash with poverty and rampant hunger, where a decent meal was a rarity and a pair of shoes was considered a luxury. This state of affairs did not lead automatically to any kind of social resistance. The Aristotelian quip that "poverty is the parent of revolution and crime" is indicative of the way in which a social crisis can drive people into a desperate fight for personal survival as quickly as it can cause them to come together. Some resorted to stealing and some to begging, while others became petty salesmen for the quacks and crooks who wished to prey upon the vulnerable and desperate. Indeed, it was not unusual for people to commit a crime for no other reason than to be placed in prison, where a meal of some sort was at least guaranteed. The journalist James Kelly recalls what Belfast was like in 1932:

> I saw naked poverty in the streets, hungry children lining up at the bakeries for so-called "cutting loaves," the stale bread returned by the roundsmen, while others clamoured at the pork shops for "griskins" and bacon clippings, or at the butchers for marrow-bones to make soup. Some, too proud to seek help from bodies like the St Vincent de Paul Society, slowly starved behind closed doors in suburban streets while unemployed husbands, shabby genteel clerks or insurance agents thrown on the scrap heap, tried to eke out a living selling shoe polish and laces from door to door in a distant part of the city where they would not be recognised. The full impact of the hard times came when unemployment benefit was exhausted and the workless came face to face with the real poverty of trying to live on "Outdoor Relief."[5]

In order to qualify for relief, the unemployed had to work on public employment schemes, performing back-breaking labor, usually on the cold, wet streets of Belfast. Thousands of people, ill-clad and ill-equipped, without proper footwear or tools, could be seen trudging through the streets, paving roads or digging up sidewalks for the slightest of remuneration, leading at times to the most tragic of consequences:

[M]en scarcely capable of lifting a heavy shovel were forced to dig roads or similar type of hard labour. I saw Harry C who had lost his job when an assurance company collapsed, working on road repairs near St Mary's Catholic Church, his thin arms and blue veins bared as he tried to wield a sledgehammer. Sweat stood out on his face as he gasped with the unaccustomed exertion. Harry had been a great man at organising amateur dramatics and he used to call at our office for a chat about the stage and players he had directed. He turned away, ashamed, as I passed. I felt for him. Harry was in his late fifties and not long afterwards I heard that he had died.[6]

Women tended to bear an even greater burden than men. Some worked—usually in the mills, where pay was much lower than the male-dominated jobs—and with a reduced life expectancy owing to the gruelling conditions of work. Still more were unemployed, but the Poor Law system did little for the workless women of Belfast. Those who were single were barred from relief, and those who were married had to rely on the relief granted to their husbands. Women who had children out of wedlock or those who had been abandoned by their husbands were left with few options. Some resorted to begging or prostitution, while others were forced to enter the workhouse, where their children were separated from them. Some hoped that the authorities would take pity on them, if only the authorities could be made aware of their suffering, as seen in this tragic letter by a woman living on the Crumlin Road in Belfast to the City Council in 1932:

> I want to see would you render me some assistance of help. I have got 2 little children, all I have to live on is 3 shillings 9 d per week health disablement, I am on lodgings, my husband has deserted my children and me and I am left with them and has [sic] got no means to live on. I am in dire want and find it very hard now the winter is coming on, I will be very thankful for anything as I am in most humble circumstances and am unable to make ends meet, hoping I shall not be forgotten in your mind.[7]

In spite of the dire straits in which many women found themselves, the Guardians did little to ease their plight. Its middle-class membership had a snobbish disregard for women, especially those with large families. In a society with few reproductive rights and a virtual absence of contraception, women were expected to "regulate" the size of their families and to ensure that they had the means to feed and clothe their children, no matter the economic circumstances. Much of this can be blamed on the sexist and conservative attitudes of a male-dominated society. However, class, as well as gender, would ultimately shape the lives of women in Belfast.

These strident restrictions on the rights of women, coupled with the ever-deteriorating economic situation, would have tragic consequences for the lives of children too. As Professor R. J. Johnstone noted, "Maternity is a more dangerous occupation in Northern Ireland than in the Free State or in England."[8] Malnutrition was rife at the time, leaving both mothers and newborns susceptible to disease or death. In 1932, Belfast alone had an infant mortality rate of 111 per 1,000 births, up from 90 in 1931 and 78 in 1930. This meant that some 11 percent of children died before their first birthdays. "There was so much infant mortality" recalled Anne Boyle, "that it seemed as if every week blue baby-coffins were coming out of every street."[9] The chief Belfast Medical Officer, Charles Thomson, described the infant mortality figures as "deplorably bad" in his annual report, and added that "the stress of the times must be held partly responsible for the high infant rate in 1932." His prognosis was stark, but his solution was in step with the rest of his class: women should simply stop having so many babies and "regulate" their families.[10]

The deepening collapse in the living standards across Belfast was dramatically transforming the social attitudes and political outlook of its population. This shift was particularly acute within the Protestant working class. The Unionist strategy had always been to maintain the allegiance of Protestant workers through a combination of preference in job allocation and relief to those deemed loyal among the unemployed. But the sheer scale of the economic crisis was ripping this strategy apart, compelling the Unionist government into an all-out class war on workers in general, without regard to creed or political allegiance. Protestants were told that they would be looked after by the state, but the reality was very different, and tensions were growing. Thomas Carnduff remembers the prevailing despondency within the Protestant working classes in this period:

> There was a despondent feeling amongst the boys. A sort of gloom-iness they had never experienced in any of the numerous pay-offs which had occurred at various periods of shipyard depression. There was none of the usual jocular remarks as to where we would spend the forthcoming holidays. . . . The optimists, and we had our full complement of them, were silent.[11]

Carnduff himself channelled his own despondency through a remarkable literary output; in 1932 he released a book of poems—*Songs of an Out-of-Work*—detailing the life and hardships of the Belfast unemployed. The *Northern Whig*, a Unionist newspaper, said *Songs of an Out-of-Work* conveyed a "bewildered resentment,"[12] a feeling not exclusive to Carnduff, who had aptly summed up the mood of his class in embittered and poetic verse:

What have we done to you,
What have we said,
That you should take from us
Our daily bread?

Are we not just as you,
Made after God,
Made in His image, if
Truthful His word?

Have we not made for you
Palace and hall,
Mansion and church for you,
At beck and call?

Fashioned the roads that you
Ride at your ease
Over the surface we
Smoothed on our knees!

Deep in the earth have we
Sweated and bled;
Slaved for your comfort
While mourning our dead.

Spade, pick, and shovel you
Loaned to us, and we
Battered our souls so that
You might be free.

What have we done to you,
What have we said,
That you should take from us
Our daily bread?[13]

Carnduff's poetry was not explicitly political, but he did capture the growing mood of discontent within the working class and the deepening sense, particularly among Protestant workers, that unionism was letting them down.

Despite the severity of the economic crisis, some working-class Protestants continued to harbor illusions that past loyalty would help them attain some sort of assistance, as shown here by a letter from an ex-member of the British armed forces pleading for help:

> I regret to have to bring my case before you. I may state that I am a disabled Ex-service man with no pension or remuneration, but quite willing to work. I may draw to your notice that I am on the O.D. Relief receiving 2 days work (ie) 16/ to maintain 6 of us in all. I may also state that I must have to keep the children home from school owing to be bare-footed and want of under-clothing and food. I am quite willing to have it put through the court as it is no fault of mine . . . I am obliged to do 2 days work weekly on the O.D. Relief which is compulsory for my livelihood and as a matter of fact I am almost on my bare feet, slushing through the water of the concrete . . . Sir if you could [kindly] assist me in any way your act would be kindly and thankfully appreciated.[14]

Another ex-serviceman from the Shankill Road who had survived the First World War describes in a letter to the Belfast Corporation his conditions, pleading for clemency on the basis of his being a "loyal man":

> Sir, Beg to inform you that I have been unemployed one year and some months and was employed in the House cleaning dept as Bin Man. I was paid of[f] through no fault of my own. I was always a loyal man having served [in the Royal Navy] and came through the war. . . . Sir I am suffering the brunt and my wife and children are in a bad way through me being unemployed. Hope Sir you will do all in your power for me.[15]

Others wrote to the lord mayor of Belfast, Sir Crawford Mc-Cullough, hoping that their loyalty as Unionists would court them some favor. Indeed, McCullough would receive letters from people who had campaigned for his election, hoping that he would reciprocate the allegiance that they had shown to him by helping to ease their plight:

> Sir, I take the liberty of writing to you on behalf of my son who is unemployed and has been for the past seven months. I am member [sic] of Ormeau Unionists and worked for you at the election you fought here and there was no one more delighted than I was when you confounded all your enemies and became Lord Mayor of Belfast and if you could do anything for my son I would be deeply grateful.[16]

Despite their efforts, neither the ex-servicemen who had survived the war nor the woman who had loyally campaigned for Mc-Cullough received anything more than a standard typewritten letter from his secretary rejecting their request.[17] Not every politician was blind to the growing crisis, however. At a special meeting of the Belfast Corporation convened to discuss the city's deepening unemployment crisis on Friday July 15, 1932, independent unionist alderman John Nixon rose to tell those in attendance that there would be a "very big reaction in this city before the 1st of November if something is not done to relieve the unemployed."[18] Nixon, representing the working-class district of Woodvale, was articulating what most poor and working-class people already knew—the unemployment situation was becoming desperate. It might have been expected that such a stark warning, coming as it did from a representative of a mainly Protestant district, would have moved the Unionist Party into action, prompting them to adopt reforms if for no other reason than to guarantee social stability. It had been clear to all that the Unionist government had until now approached the unemployment situation with detachment. What Alderman Nixon was telling them was that they could no longer continue in the same vein: if they did not act now, they would pay later. The message to the government could not have been any clearer.

Unionism was abandoning its most ardent and loyal supporters. Some elements in the Unionist establishment recognized this and were becoming anxious about the unemployment crisis. In a memorandum to the cabinet in July 1932, government minister Richard Dawson Bates outlined the two alternatives available to the state in dealing with the unemployment problem—either make concessions or prepare the state's repressive forces for the prospect of rebellion. "I do not desire to take an unduly alarmist view," he wrote, "but there can be no doubt that unless some ameliorative measures are adopted there will be a large body of the population driven to desperation by poverty and hunger, and the only alternative to Relief measures is to keep order by force, and for this purpose, in the face of widespread discontent, the existing force is not adequate . . . the situation is rapidly approaching a crisis."[19]

Despite government concern about the possibility of unrest, the official organs of the labor movement, both political and industrial, were in no mood for a sustained fightback. The trade union movement had done little to organize the unemployed and was still shell-shocked from the collapse in their membership brought on by the Depression. Representatives of the NILP had spoken with passionate outrage against the government but did little to organize on the streets. It was within this political vacuum that the meager forces of the revolutionary Left emerged, coalescing around the Revolutionary Workers Groups.

The RWGs were a small Irish Communist grouping, formed in 1930 with the backing of the Soviet Union and its international network, the Comintern. Their origins lay in the fractious period of the 1920s, when numerous attempts were made to congeal the disparate elements of the Irish Left into a viable Communist Party. A mass party of the size and influence the Comintern envisioned had by this stage been built in most other European countries, but in Ireland the gestation period had been much longer and was punctuated by a series of stillborn births and arcane splits. The first attempt was the Communist Party of Ireland, launched in 1921 by Roddy Connolly, son of the famous Edinburgh-born socialist executed by the British after the Easter Rebellion. The early Communist Party floundered from the outset, and in January 1924 was liquidated at the behest of the Comintern. In its place, the Soviets shifted support to the Irish Workers' League, led by Jim Larkin, whose stature as a legendary leader of labor, it was hoped, would draw the kind of support needed to build a mass party. Building a political party around a single individual (even one as charismatic and respected as Larkin) came with significant difficulties. Larkin proved to be a difficult individual to work with, falling out on numerous occasions with the Comintern over matters both political and personal. His forceful personality and temperamental demeanor, which had at times lent themselves to his abilities as a mass agitator, were less amenable to the minutiae of party building and internal diplomacy. Larkin, one biographer argues, "had no wish to form a party over which he would not have absolute control," and his "jealousy and possessiveness" stunted the growth of a genuine party leadership.[20] Whether Larkin's fault or not, the Irish Workers' League turned out to be "an even greater disappointment" than the failed Communist Party, and relations between the Comintern and Big Jim soured, eventually leading to a parting of ways.[21]

A more successful effort at kick-starting Irish communism was made in 1930. In March, with the help of the British Communist Bob Stewart, the "Preparatory Committee for a Workers Revolutionary Party in Ireland" was formed. Renamed the RWGs soon after, the group linked up with a small branch of Belfast Communists active in the city since the 1920s, who sent three representatives to its inaugural meeting: Tommy Watters, Loftus Johnston, and Tommy Geehan. The RWGs were small—according to a report by An Garda Síochána, the police force in the Irish state, they had as few as seventy-three members across Ireland.[22] Against the backdrop of the growing economic recession, however, the organization soon scored some successes. One of its first initiatives was to launch the Irish National Unemployed Movement (INUM), a national campaign group for those out of work. In March 1930, some ten thousand people attended INUM rallies in Dublin, Belfast, and Coleraine.[23] Encouraged by these turnouts, three Communist candidates stood in Belfast in the Poor Law guardian elections in June 1930, wining 1,183 votes between them—a modest success for an organization standing as Communists on a limited franchise (only ratepayers could vote). Through this unemployment agitation the RWGs steadily expanded, with around two hundred members nationally, thirty of whom were based in Belfast. By July 1932, its paper, the *Irish Workers' Voice* (later *Workers' Voice*), had a circulation of 360 in Belfast, along with 427 in the whole of the North and a further 995 in the South.[24]

Despite its initial success, not everyone was convinced that the RWGs were capable of leading a rebellion of the unemployed. There was good reason to be skeptical: although the unemployed of Belfast made up a large proportion of the city's population, they were completely nonunionized, scattered, and disorganized. And, of course, religious sectarianism was never far from the surface either. Communal tensions were particularly bad in the summer of 1932 in the run-up to the Eucharistic Congress (an important event in the calendar of Catholics) that was due to be held in Dublin that year. Problems began when loyalists protested at the fact that some city councillors would be attending the event as representatives of Belfast City Council. A meeting of the Belfast County Grand Lodge of the Orange Order on May 26 passed the following resolution that was sent to the lord mayor: "We feel that the presence of these aldermen and councillors in their attire will be taken as an indication that Protestant Belfast is Weakening in its attitude to the idolatrous practices and beliefs of Rome."[25] On June 25 and 26, thousands of Catholic pilgrims returning from the Eucharistic Congress in Dublin were set upon by a mobs of hundreds of loyalists when they got off the train, with sustained rioting ensuing throughout the evening in Belfast city center. It was a stark reminder of the dangers of sectarianism.

The Communists also faced opposition from organized forces within loyalism, particularly those grouped around the Ulster Protestant League (UPL), which opposed any moves to unite Catholics and Protestants and sought to "safeguard the employment of Protestants."[26] The UPL was as viciously anticommunist as it was anti-Catholic, and it would often violently attack meetings of the RWGs and the unemployed—forcing the Communists to organize security at many of their meetings—particularly around the shipyard district of Ballymacarrett in East Belfast, as reported by a historian of communism in Ireland: "On one occasion in September [1931] communists and UPL supporters fought running battles along Templemore Avenue which only ended when the police batoned the communists off the streets. Tom Watters, a future general secretary of the Irish Communist Party, and Captain Jack White, who had moved to Belfast to work with the RWGs, were both jailed for a month."[27]

The RUC kept a watchful eye on the Communists. In 1930 the Communists launched their paper, the *Irish Workers' Voice*. The RUC considered its content "inflammatory" and suggested to the government that it should be "a matter of consideration whether we should prohibit its circulation."[28] By 1931, however, alarm had abated and the RUC was confident enough to inform the government that the *Irish Workers' Voice*—described in various reports as a "miserable production "that was "on its last legs"—was "getting smaller almost weekly & will probably fizzle out before long."[29]

Within much of the Unionist state, an arrogant snobbery prevailed with regard to the prospects for a movement. RUC intelligence reports on the movement gave little cause for concern, strengthening the view within the establishment that the poor, uneducated, and unemployed of Belfast were incapable of posing a challenge to the status quo. The complacency generated by this bias was clearly revealed in a secret police report to the Ministry of Home Affairs on the launching of the Belfast branch of the Irish Unemployed Workers Movement in 1930:

There were about 100 persons at the meeting, most of them being of the low working class type, and many of them looked as
if they had never done any honest work. From their appearance
and standing it is thought that the organisation will be short-
lived. There is no doubt that it is in reality a Communist organisation . . . However they command no influence and have no
standing, therefore they need not be taken seriously.[30]

From the ragtag "low working class" ranks of this grouping, one
individual would emerge with the ability to lift the fighting spirits
of the unemployed and transform them into a formidable force. His
name was Tommy Geehan, a thirty-one-year-old unemployed la-
borer from Belfast. Described by James Kelly as "a kind of workers'
Robespierre," Geehan would become crucial to the development of
the unemployed movement in the city.[31] While he was a margin-
al figure in the wider schema of politics, Geehan's emergence as a
mass agitator was not all together unexpected. In the words of a
police report, he was a known "troublemaker" and had been active
in radical politics in Belfast for over a decade.[32] Rumors abounded
that he was a Communist, while others speculated that he was once
an IRA member. Both of these claims were in fact true. By his own
admission, Geehan had joined the IRA in 1919 in his teens and
was likely therefore to have been active in the War of Independence.
He left the republican movement in 1923, citing the creation of the
Free State for his departure.[33] In 1924 he joined the NILP in Belfast,
quickly becoming one of the party's most respected activists. Geehan's radical outlook, however, was at odds with the reformist and
respectable approach favored by many of his Labour comrades. It
was his revolutionary politics that first brought him to the attention
of the RUC—when they investigated him for making a "seditious"
speech at a West Belfast Labour Party meeting in 1927. Geehan was,
according to the RUC, a prominent public speaker who associated
"with a number of known irresponsibles" and was "only kept in check
by the more moderate opinions now prevailing in Labour circles."[34]
Under the pseudonym "Plebeian," he regularly wrote for the party
newspaper, *Forward*, where he urged the party to adopt a more revolutionary approach.[35]

Geehan became increasingly weary of the NILP's political approach and quit in 1929 when he joined the fledging forces of Irish communism. Geehan's new comrades soon sent him on a clandestine mission to Moscow to enroll in the International Lenin School, a cadre training center run by the Comintern. Geehan greatly impressed his Moscow tutors, and it was suggested that he would be suitable for full-time work in either the Communist Party itself or a trade union. It is unclear whether he took up paid party work when he returned to Belfast, though this is certainly what the RUC Special Branch speculated, and Geehan himself had declared that he was a "district organiser" in a questionnaire submitted while attending the Lenin School.[36] He stood as a Communist candidate in the June 1930 elections to the Poor Law guardians, scoring 632 votes in the Falls Ward of West Belfast. In physical appearance, at least, Geehan was a gaunt and frail figure whose "health was never robust" owing to his contraction of tuberculosis.[37] He was by all accounts, however, an orator of considerable prowess and was regularly the highlight speaker at Communist or unemployed events in the city. Geehan possessed "a powerful voice and a commanding presence," James Kelly observed. "[W]ith a mere gesture of a raised hand he could still to silence a wild and angry tumult . . . Poverty and unemployment were the fuel that would fire the class struggle in Belfast, but it was Tommy Geehan who would come to light the spark."[38]

Throughout 1932, with Geehan spearheading the campaign, the RWGs had stepped up agitation around the unemployment question. They held regular street meetings, on the dire situation facing the unemployed, every Wednesday and Friday at Exchange Square, and they had made a number of contacts among Belfast's army of unemployed. Realizing that the time had come to move beyond their usual routine of small agitational meetings, the RWGs determined to seize the moment, and in an article written by Tommy Geehan in their paper on July 2 they argued that the time for a mass movement of the unemployed had arrived:

> Poverty is rampant in the Six-Counties. Thousands are living in a state of destitution. Over every working-class home hangs the

grim shadow of unemployment and economic insecurity. Thousands face the future with black despair, frightened with the prospect that the future holds. . . . The Six-Counties workers cannot
afford any more reductions in their conditions of living. . . . The
system of private ownership and the Empire is good for the few
hundred parasites who have accumulated the mass of wealth
during years that section after section of workers were having their
wages reduced. . . . The Northern workers are not going to stand
any further reductions in their standard of living. The creation of
an unemployed organisation that will mobilise the widest mass
of workers to resist the coming attack is of supreme importance.

The Workers will fight if given the lead and the organisation to fight. The Northern Government with its £6000 per year
Prime Minister must be shown quite definitely that the workers
are standing for no more economic measures which condemn
thousands of men, women and children to slow starvation.[39]

The RWGs decided to test the water, calling a rally for July 17,
1932, at the Custom House steps. They invited Willie Gallacher, the
renowned Scottish Communist and trade unionist, to address the
crowd. In what was at that point perhaps the largest mobilization
ever called under banner of the RWGs, fifteen hundred workers attended, confirming Geehan's argument about the potential for unemployed agitation. At the rally Gallacher called for a "revolutionary
front of the workers of North and South, both Catholic and Protestant," and Geehan announced a conference of the unemployed, from
which a militant new campaign would be launched. Coming so soon
after the Twelfth of July, when sectarianism was traditionally at its
height, the RWGs saw signs that the emerging situation would lay
the basis for a challenge to the communal divide:

A week or so ago in Belfast the Falls Road was transformed with
flags and bunting and paint. Last week the Shankill Road was
also transformed with flags and paint. . . . The flags on the Falls
Road were hauled down to face the fact that the price of the loaf
had been hauled up[.] The flags on the Shankill Road will come
down to face the fact that the mills such as Craigs are closed down
for a month[.] These attacks can and must be fought back. But in

order that the fight may be effective we must first have unity in
our ranks. The bosses . . . do not throw stones at one another. They
stick together, Protestant and Catholic, Jew and Gentile, shoulder
to shoulder. . . . . Let us take a lesson from them and establish our
class solidarity, organise ourselves on a class basis and prepare to
fight back as a class.[40]

On July 25 the Outdoor Relief Workers Committee (ODRWC)
was formed with Tommy Geehan elected chair. Its aim was to
unionize those workers who worked on Outdoor Relief schemes
and to provide a focal point for all of the unemployed, in and outside
the schemes, to become organized. In an article in the *Irish Workers'*
Voice, Geehan explained that the RWGs envisaged the campaign as
a "united front of all workers irrespective of their political connec-
tions or religious opinions" and capable of launching a "widespread
campaign against the Government." Geehan and the RWGs saw
mass action as the way to challenge the state and were scornful of
the electoral orientation of the local Labour Party: "In this situation
the Labour Party leaders and the Trades Council propose that the
workers should concentrate on capturing the Board of Guardians
next June, and when this dream is accomplished then the means
test can be administered in a humane fashion. The line of advance
against the means test and wholesale poverty is along the line of
massed militant action and not along the line of put your faith in
the ballot box."[41]

The ODRWC called its first rally at the beginning of August. Speakers included Tommy Geehan and William Boyd of the
RWGs, as well as Bob Rooney and John Campbell of the NILP.
The campaign was beginning to gain momentum, and workers'
confidence was on the rise. This changing mood among the unemployed was apparent the following day at Belfast City Hall, where
a large crowd of workers who had been engaged on ODR work
schemes arrived to be paid for the work they had carried out. This
was normal practice, and the workers usually received their money
by midday. However, on this occasion the council informed them
that they would have to wait another four hours to receive their pay,
inciting a militant response by several hundred workers who invad-

ed and occupied the municipal buildings. City Hall officials were left stunned. When a city councillor announced to the workers that despite their protests they would still have to wait until four o'clock to be paid, one worker defiantly replied, "We must have our money now and we will not leave City Hall until we get it."[42] It was the first battle of wills with the authorities, and the workers emerged victorious. This caused much consternation at the Board of Guardians a few days later, when one Nationalist member of the board was accused of inciting the actions of the workers by speaking with them. The Guardian denied this vehemently but was nevertheless removed from the meeting under the threat of physical expulsion should he refuse to comply.[43]

In the early days of the campaign the ODRWC was still dependent on a small core of individuals, most of them associated with the RWGs. They decided to call a mass meeting aimed at broadening the campaign and electing a committee of elected delegates from various relief works and from existing trade union branches. The meeting, held in the hall of the Independent Labour Party (the predecessor to the NILP) in Belfast on August 8, was packed. According to Communist reports, the mood in the room was militant and there was a palpable feeling of cross-community solidarity. The *Irish Workers' Voice* reported that "a pleasing feature of the meeting was the fine turn-out of men from the east end of the city, and when the number from Ballymacarrett was announced the applause that broke out indicated that the workers from the other parts of the city appreciated the significance of the strong representation from the supposed stronghold of Unionism. . . . The meeting showed that workers from different political and religious opinions can be drawn together in a common struggle."[44]

In a script that apologists for poverty continue to follow in our own time, local politicians had responded to growing condemnation of their treatment of the unemployed with the refrain that "there was no money left." At the meeting, Tommy Geehan made a point of replying directly to this argument: "There is sufficient money in the six counties to lift the Relief workers and the mass unemployed out of the mire of poverty. . . . We are paying £2,800,000 per year for a Government apparatus. [There is] money for war, money for a huge Government apparatus, money for the share holders of banks and big concerns[,] money for all these people but none for the Relief workers and their families. The Relief workers must give the direct answer to the argument of 'no money.' There is sufficient wealth in our midst to supply the daily needs of the workers."[45]

The meeting at the ILP hall called for a mass rally for the evening of August 18. The turnout at the rally far surpassed anyone's expectations: organizers claimed an attendance of ten thousand, and even the right-wing Unionist paper, the *Belfast Newsletter*, felt compelled to admit that at least five thousand were present. The diversity of grievances inspiring those who attended the march can be seen in the variety of banners on display: "Abolish Task Work," "A Full Day's Work at Trade Union Rates," "To Hell with Charity," "We Want Work and Wages," "Should We Starve in the Midst Of Plenty?," "United Action Is the Path to Victory." The breadth of the emerging campaign could be gauged by the composition of the platform: speakers included Alderman R. Pierce and MP Tommy Henderson (independent Unionist), Harry Diamond and James Collins (Nationalist Party), and two workers affiliated with the RWGs from the trade unions: Lily Magill from the Textile Workers' Union and William Boyd of the Irish Transport and General Workers Union (ITGWU). A clear divide was evident among the speakers, between those who saw the march as the beginning of a mass campaign and those who pushed a more cautious and conciliatory approach. Alderman Pierce told those on the march that "there is only one remedy for your plight—the ballot box," which drew a rebuke from the Communist speaker Tommy Geehan:

> I would suggest to you . . . that if you want anything done in the line of getting better conditions, then you are going to be damned foolish to wait for the next General election to do it. If you want anything done, and I defy contradiction on this, you must do it for yourselves, and the thing must be done outside the floor of the House of Commons or the Board of Guardians, it must be done with your own co-operation, with the co-operation of every section of the working class . . . My advice to you is to get on with [the] work and let the next demonstration be far larger than even this one.[46]

The RWGs were ecstatic over the turnout, describing it accurately as the "greatest working class demonstration Belfast had witnessed for years." They were right in this, but they were guilty of exaggeration in declaring that "Belfast workers have gone over the top against British Imperialism and the Craigavon Government."[47] Workers were indeed fighting against the Craigavon government, but turning this into a conscious fight against imperialism would take more than a single demonstration.

The initiative taken by the RWGs compelled other sections of the labor movement to take up the question of unemployment. Hours before the ODRWC rally, the NILP and Trades Council held a joint conference to discuss action around unemployment. According to the *Newsletter*, "The conference agreed to stand candidates, whose expenses have been guaranteed by some of the largest trade unions in the district, and . . . the object is to gain control of the Board and the Public Assistance Committee, which is responsible for the administration of transitional benefit to the unemployed."[48] Elections were not due to be held until the following year, however, and there was no doubt that there was a mood among sections of the unemployed for more immediate action, as the turnouts at the RWG protests attested.

Relations between the Communists and supporters of the NILP were often volatile, and the Trades Council conference was no different. The RWGs took their lead in this period from the Comintern, which insisted that labor parties around the world were "social-fascist." This led the RWGs to adopt a hard line against the NILP, and at the conference they denounced the "treachery" of the Labour Party: "The Trades Council and Labour Party have already shown the Northern workless that the capitalist politicians of all stripes—whether Nationalist, Unionist or Labour—while compelled by mass pressure to mouth radical phrases, regard the unemployed ferment only as a vehicle for achieving municipal and parliamentary power. . . . The struggle . . . will not be led by these gentry."[49]

The divisive attitude of the RWGs to the official organs of the labor movement could often leave the Communists isolated, and they had very little base within the trade unions in this period. But their urgency and emphasis on mass action caught the mood of a section of the unemployed in Belfast, who wanted to see something done to alleviate the pressure they were under. That said, however, the Communists themselves were unsure whether they could maintain this leading role in the movement. Indeed, even their Dublin-based general secretary, Seán Murray, suggested that the RWGs' leadership in Belfast might not be strong enough to withstand the intervention of larger forces. As seen here in an internal document sent to Moscow by Murray in September 1932:

> Our group has broken through some of its previous isolation in united front work with the unemployed masses and the workers in the trade unions . . . The reformists, independent Unionists and Nationalists were forced to come in on it. They are endeavouring to direct it along lines of their own; it will tax the capacity of our groups whose leadership is anything but strong to prevent this. All we can say at the moment is that we have got a place in the mass movement.[50]

Despite the hostile approach of the RWGs to the rest of the labor movement, the Communists continued to play a crucial role in driving the unemployed agitation across Belfast, which continued to grow as the summer months came to a close. To build on this momentum, the ODRWC called for another mass rally on August 31. In the end, around twenty thousand people attended what the *Irish Workers' Voice* described as a "mighty demonstration against poverty." The march was addressed from three platforms, and condemnation of the Guardians intensified with at least one speaker describing them as "baby murderers," a reference to the widely reported death of a child in Ballymena, who had been accidentally suffocated sleeping in a cramped bed with its parents and another child. At an inquest held the week of the rally, the coroner ruled the death accidental but placed the blame on the conditions forced upon the unemployed, which meant that they could not afford the rent for houses big enough for their families.[51]

The rally was a sign that the movement was beginning to expand beyond the relief workers and unemployed themselves—numbers were swelled by the presence of trade union delegations as well as smaller groups like the Blind Workers Organisation, who spoke from the platform and pledged their support. According to the Unionist newspaper the *Belfast Telegraph*, "A resolution was adopted pledging wholehearted support for the municipal workers in their resistance against the threatened wage reductions," and there were large contingents of municipal workers on the march. The RUC noted that the RWGs "took a very prominent part in the whole proceedings, and seemed to be the organisers of the whole show."[52]

There was a strong turnout from Protestant areas on the march. This was not, however, reflected in the music played on the day. Catholic bands, including St. John's Accordion Band, St. Kelvin's Accordion Band, and St. Malachy's Pipe Band, accompanied the march. Orange bands were invited too, including the Prince of Wales Band, the Northern Belfast Pipe Band, the Northern Pipers and Brass Band, the Willowfield Brass and Reed Band, and the Ballymacarrett Flute Band, though it was announced from the platform that they had failed to turn up.[53]

Women too joined the march in large numbers, with the *Workers' Voice* noting the sizeable contingents of women on the march: "The most remarkable feature was the large number of women and girls who participated[.] Over a thousand strong they marched behind one of the textile banners, singing and cheering."[54] The women directed particular scorn at Lily Coleman, chairperson of the Board of Guardians, by chanting "We will hang Lily Coleman on a sour apple tree."[55] Coleman had always been detested in working-class areas for her treatment of those unemployed who came before the board when applying for relief. On one infamous occasion, she told a man with a large family that if the poor worked as hard looking for work as they did under the blankets there would be less of an unemployment problem, to which the man replied, "Look, Mrs. Coleman, it's fuck or freeze in this climate."[56]

Tommy Geehan closed the demonstration with a reminder of the human consequences of unemployment:

> For the last seven months over 600 children died before they reached the age of one year, died from pure starvation. . . . And the death rate during the next six months will be much higher. Day

after day workers are losing their unemployment benefit. Married workers are compelled to face the "Colemans" the "Gibbs" the "Diamonds" and the "Wilsons" and bear all their insults and abuse they can pour on them, answer the most degrading of questions in order that they may get some small Relief for their children. Day after day, men, women, and children are being driven to a premature grave, deprived of the very necessities of life, murdered.[57]

As anger continued to rise and agitation on the streets expanded, the confidence of Labour politicians in challenging Unionist dominance grew more apparent. The Unionist Party was on the rocks and the NILP was eager to use the situation to its advantage. One of the more audacious examples of this was Labour politician Harry Midgley's challenge to Unionist councillor Joseph Cunningham for an open electoral contest, which if accepted would test the level of support for the Unionist Party in the working-class Dock Ward, which they both represented. Cunningham had recently been at the center of an attempt by Unionists to pitch the unemployed against workers by suggesting that relief was so low because wages were so high, but their plan had backfired. Midgley was not shy of initiatives that bestowed attention upon himself, but a challenge like this had been unthinkable even a year previously, and it was testament to the degree to which even the usually cautious NILP was prepared to take on the might of official Unionism.

To publicize his challenge, Midgley distributed thousands of leaflets, door to door, across the area. This enraged Cunningham, and a debate ensued between the two in the pages of the *Belfast Telegraph*. Cunningham declared that he was satisfied that he was "representing the views of the majority of the working-class electors of the Dock Ward when I supported the recommendations of the Committee to negotiate a reduction of wages and salaries." Despite his claims, Midgley replied, the councillor was completely out of touch with his constituents: Cunningham's "plea that he supported the wage reductions in order to help those who are claiming Outdoor Relief would be laughable if it were not so pitiable," he wrote. "The idea of helping the poor by seeking to make poor workers still poorer is a strange doctrine and it is repudiated by the Outdoor Relief workers themselves." Knowing he had a very significant chance of being defeated, Cunningham rejected the challenge, declaring the whole controversy the result of his opponent's "overweening vanity," to which Midgley wryly replied, "I am more concerned to lift up the poor and champion the oppressed than I am with my seat, that is why I was prepared to risk it in a fight; and yet withal, I am a modest young man."[58]

As politicians bickered over the unemployment question, the unemployed themselves were busy expanding their campaign. Street meetings were held across the city throughout the month of September, including a rally attended by hundreds, mainly women, at Whiterock Crescent in the predominately Catholic West Belfast and another, addressed by Tommy Geehan, and attended by some seven hundred people, on the predominately Protestant Newtonards Road.[59] According to internal RWG documents, the ODRWC grew to ten locally organized groups across Belfast.[60]

Despite this growing unrest, the Board of Guardians would not concede. On August 23, two Nationalist Guardians proposed that the scale of relief per head should be increased to seven shillings. In proposing the motion they argued that "there seemed to be a mistaken idea that they were there to serve the rate payers only . . . the relief of the distress ought to come first."[61] Unfortunately, the rest of the Guardians did not share this sentiment, and the motion was defeated by seventeen votes to four. Following this, another motion was put to the board on September 6, this time to increase the rate per head to five shillings. Despite the measly scale of the increase proposed, the majority of the Guardians still refused to budge, and the motion was defeated by fourteen votes to eight.[62]

The prospect of the coming winter weather did not move the Guardians into action either. On September 16, it was proposed to create a one-off grant of ten shillings to the unemployed, to be paid in cash, by way of a winter allowance for coal, rent, and clothing. Again the motion was defeated, by twenty votes to four.[63] The Unionist government was as inactive as the Guardians in trying to alleviate the problem. On the same day, representatives of the Guardians met with Richard Dawson Bates, the minister for Home

Affairs, to suggest "that the government should take over the full control" of the administration of relief to the unemployed. Bates said he would consider the matter, but no official reply was ever received.[64] It was clear that the Unionist administration was happy to hide behind the Board of Guardians in order to deflect from its own shortcomings in helping the unemployed.

Pressure was now mounting on the Guardians to meet a delegation of the ODRWC to discuss the situation, but the board steadfastly refused. In light of this, the ODRWC called for a mass march on the workhouse where the Guardians were based, in an effort to force them to negotiate. The police blocked the entrance to the workhouse, and a letter was presented to them outlining their demands. The *Newsletter* reported on its contents:

> A letter received from the Committee stated that at a meeting in the Grosvenor Hall a number of demands were drawn up to be forwarded to the Guardians. Among the demands were the abolition of task work; an increase in the scale of Outdoor Relief, the increase to be to 15shillings 3d for men, 8s for wives and 2s for children and that this scale be applied irrespective of any other income of the applicant; the abolition of the system of payment in kind, and the payment to be made in money; and trade union conditions and rates of pay for street improvement work under the Poor Relief Exceptional Distress Schemes.[65]

The refusal of the Guardians to meet the workers gave credence to the view that more militant action was needed. A mass meeting was called to discuss just that.

The unwillingness of the establishment to effectively deal with the unemployment problem was creating problems elsewhere. The Northern Ireland Parliament had not met in four months and was due to reopen on September 30. However, it was decided that the Parliament would open for just a single session to discuss a solitary motion from the government before closing again for another two months. The session would take place in the Reception Room of Belfast City Hall, as the new Parliament buildings at Stormont were not yet ready. The layout of the room was carefully thought out, with the government sitting on one side, a small grouping of opposition MPs gathered adjacent, and the Speaker of the House sitting in the middle in an elevated chair above the parliamentary mace.

On the appointed day, the meeting became the site of an extraordinary scene completely out of character for the usually sedate, even sleepy operations of a one-party state. Immediately on the speaker's announcing the customary "Order, order" to begin proceedings, the NILP MP for Pottinger Jack Beattie rose to a point of order. Beattie wished to raise a motion about unemployment that he had placed before the House. The government was in no mood for a public debate over unemployment, however, and, despite Beattie's protests, the speaker deemed the motion out of order. This caused Tommy Henderson, an independent MP for the Shankill, to rise in support of Beattie. Pointing out that he had raised a similar motion before the recess that had not been discussed because Parliament had been adjourned for four months, Henderson argued that the failure to meet "was a disgrace while starving people had to suffer and the unemployed were left to their own resources." But his speech became inaudible because of shouts from the government benches. "The motion I put on the table of the House," Henderson declared, "has been lost and nobody knows anything about it. Could that happen anywhere else?" This brought a stern reprimand from the speaker, who rose from his seat, declaring it out of order for either Henderson or Beattie to continue and insisting that they sit down while he was on his feet. In violation of any sense of democratic procedure the speaker ruled that "it is for the Government whether they prorogue or continue," a maneuver that incensed Beattie, who now rose to his feet and shouted at the speaker, "I absolutely refuse to sit in this House of hypocrisy and indulge in hypocrisy with starving thousands around me." The *Belfast Telegraph* described the scene which followed: "To the astonishment of the House, Mr. Beattie rushed forward, and lifting the Mace, the emblem of the dignity of Parliamentary procedure, flung it the length of the House along the carpeted floor," yelling: "Out of the road with this; it is only the emblem of hypocrisy. I will not stand here and allow it to continue."

The mace smashed to the floor near the speaker, shocking the

House and outraging the conservative media, whose greatest concern in all this seemed to be whether the "beautiful and delicate workmanship" of the mace might be damaged beyond repair. Beattie was thrown out of the House to cries from government benches of "God Save the Queen," to which Henderson shouted back, "God Save the People." Before leaving the House in solidarity with Beattie, Henderson asked those present "what the unemployed were going to do for the next two months" while Parliament was again adjourned. He got no response from the politicians gathered inside, but in a meeting being held not far from City Hall, the unemployed of Belfast would answer the question decisively.[66]

Not long after Beattie had taken hold of the parliamentary mace, a mass meeting organized by the ODRWC was beginning. The refusal of the Guardians or the government to act to alleviate the unemployment problem was radicalizing large sections of Belfast's unemployed, and to plot a course ahead, a mass meeting had been called in North Belfast Mission Hall in York Street. Thousands of workers attended, with the Nationalist newspaper the *Irish News* reporting on a "wild scene of enthusiasm":

> Amazing scenes occurred at a meeting of almost 2,000 Relief workers . . . on Thursday night, when by an overwhelming majority, they decided to strike from all Relief schemes in the city on Monday morning. The decision was arrived at amidst vociferous cheering from the men, who packed every inch of the hall. Remarkable enthusiasm marked the proceedings, and the speakers [*sic*] addresses were frequently punctuated by uncontrollable cheering, which at times threatened to become uproarious.[67]

Tommy Geehan chaired the meeting and argued that the refusal of the Guardians to receive a delegation two days previously proved that the campaign needed to be escalated. He rose to put the ODRWC recommendation to the meeting: "The decision of your committee, which you are now asked to endorse, is that there be strike action from Monday morning." The motion's announcement was met by cheering across the hall. Not all those present, however, viewed the spectre of strike action with relish. Reverends J. N.

222

Spence and John W. Stutt, who ran the North Belfast Mission Hall, condemned the course of action, calling on workers to postpone the strike. "We believe you have an unanswerable case when you claim for better treatment," Spence argued. "I know a certain course is being advised by your committee, but I ask you not to jeopardise your cause by precipitate action." He went on to argue that the workers should have faith in the "many forces working on your behalf," to which an audience member retorted, "What about the forces working against us?" Reverend Stutt insisted that "the meeting should not take such drastic action as that proposed," advising that "for your own sake [you should] delay action until the great forces working on your behalf get properly moving."

After the clerics had finished their remarks, Tommy Geehan rose to tumultuous applause, arguing that the motion should be put and accepted. He argued that workers would not be alone, as even the clerics had conceded that they "will have the mass of the workers behind them in the strike." Stutt proposed a rival motion that called for any decision on calling action to be deferred, but it was met by uproar in the hall: cries of "We want immediate action" were chanted across the room. At this point the Reverend Stutt shifted from the conciliatory approach he had been pursuing and grew angry, declaring that if "he had contemplated the possibility of such drastic action being decided upon at that meeting he should not have given facilities for holding it in the hall."[68]

The clergy had portrayed themselves as friends of the unemployed, though it seems they were not wholly honest with those in attendance about their underlying motives. Reporting on the activities of the unemployment movement in a secret memo to the Ministry for Home Affairs, the inspector general of the RUC revealed the real intentions of the ministers in calling the meeting: "These gentlemen are alive to the fact that there is a communist element behind the Relief workers, and they are endeavouring to bring about a settlement so as the organisation will not resort to the unconstitutional acts committed in Birkenhead and Liverpool."[69] The English town of Birkenhead on the Mersey had been the scene of widespread violence between police and protesters marching under the banner of the National Unemployed Workers' Movement. Local papers had been full of reports of the march. Some ten thousand demonstrators had been baton-charged by the police, and more than one hundred fifty people were taken to the hospital, with one later dying of his injuries. Outrage at the attack on the protest provoked larger demonstrations in cities such as Liverpool, Glasgow, and Newcastle. It was clear that elites in Belfast feared that similar unrest could spread to their city.

However, the clerics' plan had completely backfired, and Stutt was met by cries of "Birkenhead," while "disorder continued in various parts of the hall for some time."[70] The significance of the "Birkenhead" chants could not be lost on anyone in the room: to cry "Birkenhead" was to exclaim that the workers of Belfast were prepared to fight in the same way, and the significance was not lost on the RUC. The inspector general warned the minister for Home Affairs that "the incidents at Birkenhead and Liverpool have given new courage to the Movement here, and while no trouble is anticipated at present, it is possible that some of the irresponsibles may endeavour to create it."[71]

In the middle of the uproar in the hall Tommy Geehan rose to finally put the motion to the vote. Amid cheering and jubilation, hands shot up in every part of the hall, and an overwhelming majority carried the motion. Geehan then announced that meetings would be held on Monday morning and marches would take place across the city to make sure that the strike call was heeded, and he declared that a support fund would be opened up to support the strikers. "We hope," he concluded, "to have up to 50,000 workers behind us."[72] The die was cast, and the battle lines were drawn—the unemployed of Belfast were up for a fight.

Chapter 4

THE OUTDOOR RELIEF STRIKE

On Monday, October 3, 1932, around two thousand workers engaged on some fifty ODR labor schemes downed their tools and ceased work. The demands of the strike were:

1. Abolition of all task work
2. An increase in the scale of Outdoor Relief to 13s 3d per week for a man, 8s a week for his wife, and 2s for each child
3. The replacement of payment in kind by payment in cash
4. The payment of any street improvement work under ODR schemes at trade union rates
5. The extension of ODR to unemployed people[1]

Picket lines were set up across Belfast to ensure that support for the action on the work schemes was solid. While the strike would be the focal point of the campaign, the workers and the ODRWC were well aware that downing tools would not be enough to beat the government. After all, the work schemes they had been engaged on were menial and unimportant, and the strike could neither harm corporate profits nor disturb the day-to-day functions of the state. If the workers remained isolated, the government would simply sit the strike out, biding its time until the pangs of hunger compelled the men back to work. It was understood from the beginning, therefore, that if the strike were to have any impact it would have to win broad support and active solidarity from other workers. The sentiment was certainly there among Belfast's working class, and the strike demands resonated not only with the thousands of unemployed and their families but with many of those still in work, who were never too far from the breadline themselves. The strike was understood not as the end, but a means to the end—a focus around which wider layers of the working class could rally. Like the story of the slave who caused a rebellion by declaring "I'm Spartacus," the workers undertook action in the hope that thousands more would be inspired to take a stand alongside them. It was in the relationship between Belfast's militant minority and the city's broader working class that the hope of victory lay. Betty Sinclair, a twenty-two-year-old fledgling Communist and linen worker who had joined the RWGs in 1932, remembered later how the ODR strike permeated generational divides as well as religious ones:

> The relief workers decided on strike action for October 3, 1932. Now I always remember it very, very vividly because my father was unemployed at the time and I also was unemployed. When I was going out of the house that morning to speak at my first public meeting on the relief workers' issue in Library Street, I said to my father. "I don't know what will happen, whether I'll come home tonight or whether I will be [in] jail." My father said, "Remember, the door is always open."[2]

Using the strike to build a mass movement was central to the ODRWC's strategy from the beginning. On the first morning, having ensured that the work schemes were not running, the workers set off visiting working-class districts and workplaces in the city in order to build support. At various locations they would stop and hold impromptu meetings, usually on empty land, calling on locals to come out and hear their case. It was a highly successful tactic. As the workers went from district to district their numbers swelled, with thousands of supporters joining them, marching through the city in jovial procession, backed by throngs of new recruits and cheered and applauded by crowds lining the streets. Although there was a large presence of police on standby, the *Belfast Telegraph* reported that "everything was perfectly orderly," noting that the organizers had taken "every precaution to avoid disturbance of any kind."[3] By sunset the march had grown to a colossal size, led through the streets by a bright line of torchbearers, slowly progressing en masse toward a planned rally at the Custom House steps. The *Irish News* described it as "one of the largest demonstrations in the history of the city":

> There was no mistaking the strength of solidarity in the crowds which thronged the streets. Royal Avenue was one dense mass of people.... Rarely had Belfast witnessed such a gathering of people in its main thoroughfare. It was impossible to move on the footpaths. The roadway was a swaying mass of people, crushing, pushing around the stationary lines of tramcars, motorcars and lorries. Women with babies in their arms and young children fought their way through to see the demonstrators, who marched along, carrying torchlights, singing and cheering.... The crowds swept along the streets in solid mass, controlled by its own force of numbers. At some places children were in danger of being crushed, but groups of young men, joining hands, cleared a passage for them.[4]

The crowd at the rally was so big—at least sixty thousand—that the majority of people could not hear the main platform, and more than a dozen impromptu meetings had to be organized in the vicinity on at least eight hastily erected platforms.[5] There was a wide range of speakers, including Communists, Nationalists, independent Unionists, and NILP members. From one platform, NILP MP Jack Beattie called on Protestant working-class districts to refuse to decorate their houses with flags and bunting during the forthcoming visit of the Prince of Wales in protest of the unemployment situation. "[A] loaf of bread on the workers' breakfast tables," he said "was the best decoration for them."[6] A speaker from the ODRWC declared that if the strike lasted longer than a week they would call for a strike of schoolchildren in order to shut down the education system. He also called for a non-payment campaign to landlords and the "tick" men until the strike was over—a hugely popular proposal in a city where most people could only afford to have furniture by renting it from "tick" men who went door to door every week collecting payments. He urged those gathered not to worry about eviction for non-payment of rent, as "heaven help the man who tried to put them out."[7]

A number of Communist speakers—Tommy Geehan, Betty Sinclair, Arthur Griffin, and Seán Murray—spoke for the RWGs from one platform or another. The Communists used their time on the platforms to raise anti-sectarian politics and to call for an escalation of action. Some speakers had alluded to the possibility of a compromise with the Guardians and the government, but the revolutionaries were in no mood for acquiescing. The final speaker that day was Tommy Geehan. As he stood on the platform at the Custom House steps, peering over the sea of people amassed in the square, he might well have been struck by how far they had come from that first rally in July. He reminded the crowd that just a few months ago the unemployed of Belfast "had been divided by artificial barriers of politics and religion, but tonight they had Protestants from the Shankill Road and Catholics from the Falls Road marching shoulder to shoulder." The energy and unity on display that night could not be allowed to dissipate, he argued, and with a passionate urgency he called on the unemployed to keep up the fight:

> We have got to go round, and make a collection from door to door, from corner to corner, because this is a very serious fight we have embarked upon. If the Relief Workers are beaten, then all I can say is "Heaven help the destitute workers of Belfast this winter." If we are beaten now, the Guardians will further cut the scale of Relief, they will become more brutal in their attitude to you and yours. . . . Consequently, we have got to win, and not to ask ourselves "Can we win?" We must win! We must have more of the spirit of Birkenhead and Invergordon,[8] we have got to get results in this desperate fight, we have got to win, and no matter what the costs or sacrifices may be, we will win.
>
> Fellow workers, we have got to win this fight, if we don't win it, the future will only hold for us the same mass misery, mass poverty and mass destitution. If we don't lift sufficient money to feed the wives and kiddies of the strikers in the Relief Workers, then we have got to remember that in this city there is plenty of food and clothes and by God we are not going to allow one of our kiddies or women to starve.
>
> It has been suggested that we are not fair in demanding action that we should have waited to allow the Guardians to consider our case. Well for the past number of years "task work" has been our portion. Deputation after deputation went to the Guardians.

What was the answer of the Guardians? Every appeal made to them and based on humanitarian grounds was refused. The only way to make these people recognise the destitution that exists is the way we have taken, and if the strike lasts over the week we have got to realise and consider what our next step is going to be. If the Guardians don't give concessions by the methods we are using, then we have got to take other methods and wring from them concessions, and we are going to do it.[9]

Geehan then turned to practical plans for the next week:

Now if the strike goes into next week, we are calling a strike of the school children[,] we will ask the parents of these school children not to send them to school next week for as long as the strike lasts. [*Cheers*] And on the question of Rent, individually my advice to you is to pay no rent, no rent is to be paid until the strike is over [*loud cheers*] or pay no tick-men [*cheers*]. I suggest that you don't want to pay rent, because if the strike lasts for any considerable time, and you are behind with your rent, and they attempt to evict you, Christ help the people who attempt to put you out. [*Cheers*] Not a penny of rent to be paid next week and no children to be sent to school. We will have mass demonstrations, and if we do not have an answer from the Guardians before the end of the week we will have a midnight mass demonstration through the City of Belfast. Let our slogan be. "No Surrender to poverty, misery and destitution."[10]

The demonstration was an extraordinary show of strength on the part of the unemployed, and a clear signal that the movement was now of a mass character. The activity did not cease that night with the close of the demonstration. Another march later that night from Derry to Belfast, though smaller in size, poignantly illustrated the lengths to which people were going to join the campaign, reported here by journalist James Kelly:

Late at night I stood at North Street [in Belfast] and saw the arrival at the Bakers Hall of a contingent of scarecrows, a Hunger March from Derry, with tattered banners, exhausted and starving after the long hike across the bleak Sperrins and down the Glenshane Pass. There was confusion and an air of excitement as locals tried to arrange food and shake-down accommodation for the Derry men.[11]

Internal government documentation shows that both the RUC and the government in Northern Ireland were increasingly concerned that the RWGs were the "driving force behind [the] strike."[12] While it is true that the Communists were, in the main, the leading elements of the campaign, the thousands who followed them were not merely passive bystanders. As the movement grew, so too did the participation of ordinary people, infusing a sense of collective strength among the long-suffering working class of Belfast. Betty Sinclair remembered this flowering of human ingenuity. "One of the most interesting things about the whole period," she recalled, "was men and women who had never spoken on a platform in their lives became orators overnight, through sheer desperation. The talents of the people were being revealed. Everywhere people were asking questions and putting forward proposals."[13]

The day after the mass rally the strikers returned to the picket lines with plans to diversify the tactics used in the campaign. One target was the workhouse where the Board of Guardians was situated. On Tuesday, October 4, thousands of people marched on the workhouse to demand that the Guardians meet a deputation of the unemployed. When the marchers arrived they found the gates guarded by a strong force of police. Still, they were in no mood to take "no" for an answer and decided to block the roads and tram tracks until the Guardians agreed to meet them. For the next four hours the trams and road traffic in South Belfast were blocked as a "continual roar of singing, cheering and shouting" was heard through the streets.[14] Not only could traffic not move; as reported by one newspaper, the Guardians themselves were unable to leave the grounds:

> There were remarkable scenes in Belfast yesterday when thousands of men marched to the Workhouse in support of a deputation of unmarried men who claimed outdoor relief. The procession marched through the centre of the city and was watched by crowds almost as great as those of Monday night.
>
> So dense was the throng that Guardians and others going to

the Workhouse had to go round about way, and some had even to climb the railings. When it was announced to the crowd that it would be a considerable time before the deputation would return, they sat down on the roadway and sang songs, while now and again they took up the cry: "We want grub! We want work!"[15]

Inside, the Guardians debated among themselves about how to best deal with the situation. According to the meeting minutes, one member warned that if the board did not "receive these people he would live to regret it," while another said that if they did "not meet this response adequately then they were courting disaster and trouble." Eventually the board conceded, and a delegation of three unemployed protesters were allowed in. Arthur Magill, a member of the ODRWC and RWGs, told the board that "they were only asking for the right to live on behalf of the people they represented that day." However, the board was unwilling to countenance any criticism of their record. The delegation was told that they "were in the wrong place altogether" as "no person in the city of Belfast had made greater sacrifices for the unfortunate poor than the members of the Belfast Board of Guardians."[16] Nevertheless, the strikers had scored a small victory: up to that point the Guardians had refused to even consider the idea of meeting but had now been forced to accept a delegation to quell the mounting anger. The turnaround helped to magnify the sense that the campaign was gaining ground. The majority of those marching on the workhouse were single men: at the suggestion of Tommy Geehan, it was agreed that they would return the following night, with admission cards, and enter the workhouse, as was their right.[17]

The sheer size of the movement and the disruption it was creating across the city was causing deep concern in the ranks of the establishment. Among the business class—both Catholic and Protestant—there was palpable fear about the effect the new militancy might have on the economy. An *Irish News* editorial summed up the mood of the Catholic middle classes: "It is essential to tackle the problem of the unemployed, not merely for the sake of those who are out of work, but also because the affairs of business men and traders are suffering."[18]

It was becoming increasingly apparent that the state could not continue with its uncompromising approach: concessions would have to be made. Many Protestant church leaders were calling for a substantial increase in relief, though the Catholic Church remained quiet for fear of giving succor to the Communist menace. On Monday, October 3, the Belfast Chamber of Commerce agreed to "the formation of a committee to investigate the possibilities of instituting depots for the provision of food for destitute families in the poorer quarters of the city during the coming winter."[19] It was clear that this proposal did not emanate from some newfound philanthropic spirit among the wealthy—they had not lifted a finger to help feed the poor for years. Rather, local elites understood that unless something was put in place to feed the unemployed, hunger would continue to feed the mood of resistance.

There were those within the state who also understood that action needed to be taken. On Wednesday, October 5, a conference was held in Belfast City Hall to look at a possible resolution to the crisis. The meeting was a gathering of the various strands of the Northern bourgeoisie and was attended by representatives of the Northern Ireland government, the Belfast Corporation, the Board of Guardians, and key figures in industry. They committed to introducing additional distress schemes, recommended that the Board of Guardians increase the number of hours per week given to men on the exceptional relief schemes, agreed that the Corporation would begin additional unemployment relief schemes, and invited representatives of the ODRWC to City Hall to put the concession to the workers. Their sudden conversion to more flexible arrangements was a clear sign that the ODR strike was perceived as a serious threat.[20]

The ODRWC agreed to go to City Hall to hear the offer. They called for a mass meeting of the striking workers on Wednesday, October 5, in St. Mary's Hall to ensure that any offer could be swiftly put to democratic vote. Entry to the meeting was limited to the striking relief workers themselves, some four thousand of whom packed into St. Mary's Hall to await the delegation's return, after identifying themselves at the door with a red food docket they received earlier in the strike. In a testament to the strike's broad support, thousands upon thousands of people gathered outside to await the decision of the meeting: Bank Lane, Castle Street, Smithfield, and King Street were completely overflowing with people. When the delegation returned, the offer was outlined to the strikers. Two representatives from the government urged the relief workers "to give their offer a trial for a number of weeks to see how it would work out."[21]

Tommy Geehan outlined the offer to the crowd before adding that while in his view the terms of the agreement fell short, he would abide by the decision of the meeting. Geehan argued that the rate of relief was still too low and that there were no provisions in it for single men or women. When the offer was put to the floor the meeting rejected it unanimously. Attention immediately turned to practical plans for escalating the action. Proposals to organize a rent and tick strike were approved, as was a call for a school student strike the following week. Strikers agreed to immediately prepare to have "bonfires on every road in the city on Monday evening prior to Tuesday's demonstration." A mill worker announced that a delegation from their workplace would accompany the strikers on the march and that they would make sure "there would not be a mill going in the city on Tuesday evening." To cries of "Birkenhead" and "Up Russia," Geehan called for a mass rally the following Tuesday:

> "On Tuesday next, we will seek to mobilise 80,000 workers to go down to the Guardians and throw down our demands. It's going to be a fight to the finish. Also we have got to try and persuade the organised workers of the city to call a general strike for Tuesday." To wild cheers from the audience he said that if their demands were not met by Tuesday "this committee will not be responsible for the conduct of the workers."[22]

The strikers' decision to reject the offer did not go down well with the government. While the meeting was underway, large forces of policemen backed by armor-caged cars were being deployed strategically across the city: the government was preparing for a change in tactics in the event of a rejection of the conference terms. The *Irish Independent* reported that "an atmosphere of the greatest tension prevailed in the city" as groups of armed RUC stationed themselves across Belfast.[23] Unbeknownst to the strikers, the state was about to implement its contingency plan.

The tactics employed in the campaign were also escalated. Five hundred single unemployed workers had gathered in Frederick Street, having obtained cards for admission to the workhouse. However, the police informed the marchers that the demonstration was banned. David Scarborough, a speaker at the rally, summed up the mood of many:

> Two Detectives wanted to bring word here to the Committee that if these people walked in the Demonstration, tonight, that they would use force. Force. Remember that. I can tell you this, we don't want force used, not that we are afraid of force, but we don't want them using force when we can prevent it. I told the two detectives this, not in bravado. I mean every word of it, if it comes to using force we are prepared for that, and we will use force in return [*loud cheers*]. . . . We will be able to show them that we are the real ruling class, we the workers.[24]

Their plan was to then march up toward the Lisburn Road and enter the workhouse, but when they turned into York Street the police charged them violently with batons. Forced off the roads, the men walked to the workhouse in ones and twos on the footpath. But further attacks were in store. When a crowd gathered on the Lisburn Road to support the men, a large contingent of police arrived and attacked the assembly, dispersing the crowd into smaller side streets. Chaos ensued as the baton charge continued, with shouting and screams audible as people ran for cover into doorways and alleys. The majority of the scattered crowd was pushed into Sandy Row, where thousands congregated, seeking safety in numbers. The police formed lines across the road, facing the crowd with their hands on their batons: an attack was clearly imminent. Suddenly, a hail of stones and bricks came flying from the crowd into the police lines, momentarily breaching their formation and allowing many to break out of the police cordon. Windows were smashed in a number of shops, and hand-to-hand fighting erupted between the police and demonstrators.[25] Geordie Loughrey paints a vivid picture of events on Sandy Row that night:

> The action of the police in forcing people back: that started the
> riot. When we got into Sandy Row, two or three times the police
> would come swooping in, trying to chase the people away. But
> along Sandy Row the doors would open and everyone—it didn't
> matter who you were, what you were—you were just brought
> into the house. Doors closed again while the police were about.
> As soon as the police would go away again, the people all got
> out onto the road again, kicking up, shouting slogans. The police
> didn't come into the houses. That was what really surprised me, to
> tell you the truth. They did it on parts of the Falls.[26]

The violence would not be confined to Sandy Row: the thousands who had gathered inside and outside of St. Mary's Hall would
be the next targets. As the strikers were leaving the hall, a large
force of police attacked them, causing Belfast city center to descend
into a full-scale riot. As the night wore on and people moved back
into their own areas, rioting continued in the working-class districts,
particularly on the lower Falls, the Shankill Road, and Sandy Row.
The rioting, however, represented more than simple destruction of
property. Class anger permeated through much of the violence, as is
clear from this incident described by Liam Tumilson, a member of
the ODRWC and resident of the Shankill Road:

> [W]hen the demonstration was returning from the workhouses
> to the city, the Shankill heroes who were with this demonstra-
> tion, when they were marching from the workhouse on their way
> home, they heard of an eviction taking place in Percy St. They
> went round there, and found that the bailiffs already had the fur-
> niture on the van. Well they chased the bailiffs, put the furniture
> back again, turned the horse loose and smashed and burned the
> van. The bailiffs have not been heard of since.[27]

This was an important turning point: up until that moment, the
campaign for a fair deal for the unemployed had been almost entirely
peaceful. The organizers had gone to great lengths to ensure that processions were well stewarded, and calls to keep the movement peaceful
were made repeatedly from the platforms. Even the hostile Unionist

press had repeatedly highlighted the orderly nature of the campaign. There can be little doubt, then, that the impetus for violence had come from above. Having failed to stall the movement with concessions, the state decided to crush it through violence and repression.

Back at the workhouse those who had gained admission were making themselves as much of a nuisance as possible. Since they were unemployed and had obtained admission cards there were no grounds for refusing them entry, and thus around three hundred men were allowed in. Entry into the workhouse was a tactic, and the men had no intention of submitting to its strict Victorian discipline. Instead, they aimed at exposing the absurdities in the Board of Guardians' strategy. For each individual staying in the workhouse, it cost the Guardians just 16s 1d per week, considerably more than the unemployed were asking in relief, which made a mockery of the board's claim that it could not afford to pay single men relief.

Attempts were made by workhouse officials to split the men along sectarian lines. Upon entering, officials tried to separate them by putting Protestants into one ward and Catholics into another. The plan, however, did not come off, and when the first man was asked for his religion, he refused to answer, replying only "I'm destitute."[28] The men sat up all night in the workhouse singing and cheering; in the morning they refused the meager breakfast on offer and threatened to cause a commotion unless eggs were provided instead. Workhouse officials could not keep the situation under control, and the police were frequently called. The Unionist paper the *Newsletter* reported that "inside the workhouse there were stormy scenes[.] Two young men were arrested for alleged insubordination to the ward masters and ... conveyed to the central police station[.] The majority of the police on duty at the gates returned to their various depots about 9.00 p.m. but a considerable force remained inside the premises all night to cope with any trouble that might arise in the wards."[29] The Board of Guardians dismissed claims that the workhouse was being overrun, insisting that there was no specific increase in numbers in the workhouse and that "quite a normal number" had been admitted that week.[30] Their own internal figures, however, show that numbers for able-bodied males in the workhouse nearly doubled that week, the highest figure for weekly admittance that year.[31]

The following day was much quieter, with the *Irish Independent* remarking on a "marked cessation today of the hostilities," adding, however, that "there is a feeling of tension [in the city], and knots of unemployed men are to be seen along the main thoroughfares."[32] Pickets began as usual at 7:30 a.m., and strike meetings were held throughout the city. At a Shankill Road meeting, Betty Sinclair and Henry Finlay of the RWGs urged the workers to avoid riots like the one that had occurred the previous evening lest they bring further attacks from the state.

Delegations went out to the mills and factories to speak to workers, and at lunchtime workers came out to hear calls from the strikers for solidarity action the following Tuesday. Collections were held across the city in order to build up the strike fund. The police were out again in force, but no attempt was made to attack the pickets. The Trades Council also held a conference to discuss its strategy in relation to the movement, providing a crucial opportunity for the RWGs to test their strategy of building for a general strike. Communist speakers called for the unions to shut the city down on Tuesday and for mass protests to be organized against the visit of the Prince of Wales, whom they described as a "second-hand salesman of British capitalism."[33]

While the RWGs made a clear case for the general strike, they were in no position to force the union leadership into action. The Communists had very little base within the unions, and their constant attacks on the union leadership as "social-fascist"—in keeping with the Comintern's hostility toward trade union leadership—did little to gain the support of rank-and-file workers. The RWGs believed that they could completely bypass the unions and make a direct appeal to rank-and-file workers. While this approach was in many ways admirable and expressed a healthy impatience with the bureaucratic inertia of the official labor movement, it was also completely unrealistic. There was widespread support among many workers for the plight of the unemployed, but it was highly unlikely that the mass of the working class could be convinced to come out for a general strike without the support of their unions. The RWGs had no rank-and-file networks within the unions that they might work through to build for a general strike. Instead, they were reduced to making calls from outside of the major workplaces, and this marginalization placed definite limits on their ability to mobilize. As a result, union leaders felt very little pressure to call a general strike, deferring the decision to a future conference of the various trade union officials in the city.[34]

While the growing militancy was a cause for concern, the Unionist establishment remained confident that the movement was incapable of mounting a general strike. They denounced "the silly suggestion . . . that a general strike of workers of the city should be called," asserting that "such a foolish and impracticable proposal will not meet with any sympathy from the moderate section of the Trade Union leaders," and that any call would be ignored by "those who consider themselves fortunate to be in work."[35] In fact they were far more worried about the planned protests against the Prince of Wales's visit than they were about prospects for a general strike:

> Even at the Trades Council last night scurrilous and offensive observations were made about the Prince of Wales. Why bring the Prince of Wales into it? If any man deserves well of British Labour, the Prince does, because his visits abroad have resulted in orders worth millions of pounds coming to this country. The working classes have no greater friend than the Prince.[36]

As the mass demonstration on Tuesday grew closer the government made one last-ditch effort to derail the strike. On Thursday, October 6, Dawson Bates met with the Board of Guardians to pressure them into offering a new deal. On the following night the offer was put to the strikers—a 50 percent increase in the number of days that work was available, a 50 percent increase in the amount of money paid in relief, and a commitment to pay the men the money they had lost while on strike. While the offer did not meet all the demands of the strikers, it was certainly the most significant concession from the government yet. Another mass meeting was arranged for that evening in St. Mary's Hall. The offer would put to the test the will and determination of the strikers—would they accept what they were offered or hold out for more?

At the meeting in St. Mary's Hall, Tommy Geehan argued that the terms were an attempt to split the strikers: there was still no provision for single men or women, or workers with large families. He moved for the rejection of the offer, seconded by a member of the Shankill branch, and called on the workers to keep up the fight:

> Everything [is] pointing to the ultimate victory of the workers. [We have] secured a certain victory up to the present, and all [we have] got to do [is] tighten up [the] resistance and on Tuesday have every worker on the streets. Furthermore, whether or not the demonstrations are banned on Tuesday we are going to the Guardians."[37]

Geehan's intervention against the offer was crucial. His stature as a leader of the unemployed had grown immeasurably, as seen by the tribute made to him in the course of the meeting, with one speaker praising him as the individual "who had organised the movement . . . proving Comrade Geehan's power of organisation."[38] The meeting voted against accepting the government's offer—not a single hand in the hall went up to accept the terms. There were hopes that the movement would spread elsewhere, with one speaker praising the Belfast relief workers for giving a "lead to the rest of the country."[39] Various speakers rose to testify to the movement's solid support across the city, with Henry Finlay, leader of the Shankill Road group, declaring that the district was "solid behind" the movement.[40]

Tommy Geehan had stern words of warning for the Guardians should they refuse to budge: "If the Guardians still refuse to consider our demands there are five or six other tricks up our sleeves and by the end of next week we will make some of them wish to heaven they were never born."[41] The meeting agreed to go ahead with the mass rally on Tuesday, October 11, and reiterated the call for a general strike. William Boyd of the ITGWU and RWGs argued that they "could paralyse the city" if only they had solidarity. Another speaker went further, warning that if "the trade union officials did not get their men out on strike Tuesday, the Relief Workers Committee . . . would kick the officials out of the Labour movement."[42]

The workers were becoming increasingly aware of state attempts to provoke violent confrontations at protests and meetings. A police officer, sent to record the meeting, reported on Geehan's concluding remarks to the strikers:

> He understood that a number of policemen had found their way into the hall. He appealed to those present to disperse quietly and said anyone who went contrary to the instructions of the committee was not wanted. Leaving the hall the policemen may be there and may give certain amount of provocation if any but to go to your different districts and go home peacefully. He was convinced that what was to be attempted was to draw the workers into a premature attack.[43]

By Monday morning the strike was a week old, and obtaining food to feed the strikers and their families was now of paramount importance. A food depot was opened at the ITGWU headquarters on Corporation Street, and long queues formed outside of it on Monday morning. It took some hours to distribute the food to the strikers, as many people not involved with the strike had turned up in the hope of getting a free meal.[44] Other food depots were opened across the city to distribute goods donated by individuals and small shops. Horse-drawn carriages were requisitioned to deliver the food from depot to depot. The strikers themselves also took to organizing door-to-door collections in working-class districts. Through these collections the workers received 4,927 loaves, 800 stone of potatoes, 727 pounds of sugar, 170 pounds of tea, 91 pounds of butter, 131 pots of jam, and 10 stone of flour in donations.[45] Tommy Fitzpatrick described his involvement in collections in the Dock area: "I rapped on a door and I asked people—they might give you bread, milk, sugar, different things. That was people who were working; they could afford it. The Dockers were very good to us. They had a collection amongst themselves. So we were able to give out half a crown."[46]

Whether a general strike was called or not, the demonstration planned for Tuesday, October 11, was expected to be of colossal proportions. The agitation was also spreading across Ireland, sometimes through the agitation of local Communists. On September 28, some four hundred unemployed workers came together to form the Derry Unemployed Workers Movement, and on October 4, they held their first rally, where one speaker, Edward Brady, said "that there were about 800 families in dire starvation" in the city.[47] In Armagh, a deputation of the unemployed met city councillors to tell them "the position of the unemployed in the city was desperate."[48] Also, in the South of Ireland, unemployment action inspired by the events in the North was on the rise, and a series of occupations of county councils were held over the issue of relief. On October 5, a body of two hundred unemployed men, carrying banners inscribed "Why Starve in the Midst of Plenty?" and "We Want Work or Maintenance," marched to the County Sligo Board of Health offices and requested that the board provide a relief scheme equal to unemployment insurance.[49] In Kilkenny, hundreds of unemployed invaded the local council chambers to demand an improvement in conditions for the unemployed. Some of these protests grew violent. In Tralee, the unemployed marched on the local Urban Council, during which "a member of an unemployed deputation, after interchanges with the Chairman and Borough Surveyor, hurled a chair from the end of the room which crashed behind the chairman's back."[50] The RWGs also organized solidarity demonstrations in Dublin. Three workers from Belfast, all of them ex-Unionists and Protestants according to internal RWG documents, were brought to Dublin to address solidarity rallies and to meet the Dublin Trades Council.[51]

In the North, the Unionist establishment was growing increasingly worried about the movement and the role of Communists within it. "An admittedly serious state of affairs is being seized on by Socialist and Nationalist orators," the *Newsletter* warned, "not so much with the hope of discovering a practical remedy as in the hope of discrediting authorities, state and local, and of paving the way to revolutionary changes."[52]

The day before the mass rally, the *Belfast Telegraph* reported a speech by Jim Larkin Jr., "Big Jim" Larkin's son, at an RWG event in Dublin under the headline "Larkin Revelation—Object of Strikers Disclosed—To Fight British Empire and All that It Stands For."[53] Tuesday's planned demonstration was being presented to the public—and, crucially, to Protestant workers—as a combined Communist and republican plot to overthrow the government, thus creating a pretext for its violent repression. The organizers were condemned as "enemies of the state." Rev. John Spence now called for action to halt "the menacing advance of atheistic communism," while Unionist MP Herbert Dixon urged Protestants, both rich and poor, to unite to block Communist attempts to "smash the machine and throw out the government."[54]

The state was preparing its forces to crush the unemployed movement. On Monday, October 10, news broke that Dawson Bates had banned all meetings and demonstrations in the city under the Special Powers Act. It was not an unusual move for the minister of Home Affairs, described by James Kelly as a "buck-toothed . . . waspish solicitor, with a taste for the bottle [and a] white moustache stained yellow from chain smoking," who thought nothing of utilizing the sweeping "dictatorial powers" he possessed:

> [His] appearance belied his reputation as the "strong man" of the Cabinet. He was the Kremlin's Beria in local politics by virtue of his almost dictatorial powers over police, Specials, prisons, local courts and law and order . . . Bates merely had to sign his name to a piece of paper to intern anyone, hold persons for questioning, ban meetings, inquests, newspapers and gramophone records, seize property and motor vehicles and "exclude" individuals to remote areas of the North, a disguised form of deportation."[55]

The RUC was uncertain whether it could contain trouble, and Bates called in an extra seven hundred police to assist them, backed up by an additional two thousand police in armored cars—in all at least half the entire police force of Northern Ireland would be on duty in Belfast. The Royal Inniskilling Fusiliers were put on standby, and police were issued with rifles in addition to their customary revolvers. Notices were put in the press warning people not to attend the rally, and the Bishop of Down and Connor urged priests to use Sunday mass to impress upon Catholic churchgoers that confrontation with the police should be avoided.[56]

There was a palpable tension in the air in Belfast as people waited to hear the reaction of the strikers. Eight years previously the deployment of the Special Powers Act had been enough to crush the unemployment movement in an instant. In the face of repression and violence the union leaders of 1925 decided to cave and cancelled their protest. But the leadership of the unemployment movement in 1932 was of a different sort. The RWGs were not prepared to give in and hurriedly arranged meetings to assure people that the protest would go forward. Strikers held a mass meeting at the Custom House steps to discuss the demonstration. In reply to rumors that the state was planning on using the B-Specials against the demonstration, one speaker said this would be difficult and asked, "Did the government forget that there were many B-Specials in the ranks of the Outdoor Relief workers?"[57]

As ever, Tommy Geehan was at the forefront of the charge. At a mass meeting of women workers from the Belfast mills, held on the eve of the rally and organized to express support for the strike, he urged the thousands in attendance not to break the unity that they had built up between Protestants and Catholics, assuring them that the demonstration was most certainly still on:

> Whether or not the Government banned the demonstrations the workers are going out on the streets . . . the demonstration is not being held for the purpose of coming into conflict with the authorities. A peaceful and orderly demonstration of Belfast workers is going to march to the Belfast Workhouse. . . . Tomorrow you will see the mightiest demonstration of unity that has ever been seen in Belfast. The authorities have banned the demonstration tomorrow but the workers are going out . . . to the Guardians to show them that the mass of workers—organised and unorganised, employed and unemployed—are determined that we will no longer live under rotten conditions of poverty. There must be no weakening . . . the fight must go on until victory [has] crowned their efforts on behalf of the masses of suffering humanity in their midst.[58]

Despite government hopes that they could intimidate the movement off the streets, the demonstration was going ahead. Liam Tumilson warned that there might be attempts to arrest the leaders of the movement:

> Now here is the position. You have the Committees, the Outdoor Relief Committee and the Unemployed Committee, now if there

is any trouble, some of these members might be arrested. Most of you know the men who are members of these Committees. You all know Tommy Geehan is the Chairman of the Relief Workers Committee. An attempt may be made to arrest Tommy Geehan, or some other leaders. If any of the leaders are arrested there must be demonstrations held following their arrest, and let these demonstrations be orderly.

Liam Mulholland, a prominent IRA figure in Ardoyne and a member of a local Unemployed Workers Committee, later remembered that "there was no ODR man who wanted any violence" on the demonstration, but that the police clearly had other ideas.[59] The state was preparing to violently crush the movement, but it would not be as straightforward as they expected. Over the weeks and months the unemployed of Belfast had grown more militant, more cohesive, and more sure that the fight they were engaged in was right and just. They had built up a momentum and would not easily give up the fight.

A small story in the *Belfast Telegraph* on the morning before the demonstration summed up the situation among the destitute of Belfast. A man was hauled before the court, having been arrested in Castle Street for breaking a window in plain view of a policeman. When asked by the judge to explain his action, he explained, "I broke the window because I was hungry. Jail is the only place where I can get food."[60] The unemployed of Belfast would not be easily intimidated: they had nothing to lose and everything to gain.

Chapter 5

THE ODR RIOTS: BELFAST'S "FESTIVAL OF THE OPPRESSED"

On the evening of Monday, October 10, 1932, the streets of Belfast were tense with anticipation. It was the eve of the banned mass rally that was set to take place in the city the following day. No one was quite sure what to expect, but a showdown was certain.

That night, the RUC patrolled working-class districts of Belfast, as groups of men and women gathered at street corners in anticipation of the bonfires that were to take place across the city. The police confiscated any materials deemed to be of use in building a fire and immediately removed them to Brown Square Barracks. Still, crowds gathered in defiance of the police. On the Falls, a bonfire was erected with a collection of old boots, bicycles, disused articles of clothing, and motor tires. As soon as it was lit, the police emerged with buckets of water to extinguish it: abuse was hurled from the crowd but no one dared relight the fire. The police didn't have such an easy time in the working-class Protestant districts of Belfast, where the lighting of bonfires was a deeply engrained tradition. Extensive preparations had been made on the Shankill and several bonfires were lit in the district. Small-scale rioting occurred on the road as youths pelted police with stones when they attempted to extinguish the bonfire. It was a frustrating night for the police—as soon as they extinguished one fire, another one was lit, and youths and police engaged in a cat-and-mouse game throughout the night.[1]

The Shankill was not the only scene of violence that evening. At around eight o'clock, a large crowd assembled in Cromac Square for a street meeting organized by members of the RWGs. Minutes into the meeting, the police forced their way into the crowd and arrested the speaker, twenty-one-year-old Maurice Watters of Fairview Street. Stones were thrown at police, and windows were smashed as rioting ensued in the area for the next few hours. By midnight, the police had extinguished all but a few bonfires, and many people took to parading through their local areas instead. Throughout the night large gatherings of young men and women marched through the streets singing "We Want Bread" and "Up to the Union We Will Go" to the tune of popular songs at the time. The evening's low-level violence was a foretaste of what was to come. By early morning the police reported to the press that all was quiet across the city: it was the calm before the storm.[2]

The mass march was scheduled for around lunchtime that day. One person who would certainly not be marching was Watters, who was brought before the courts that morning. The fact that he was a speaker at the Cromac Square meeting was enough for the police to finger him as ringleader, a clear signal that the state intended to target leading figures in the movement. Watters was charged, preposterously, with incitement to murder John Wilson and Lily Coleman, both members of the Board of Guardians, on the grounds that he had made a speech in which he'd allegedly remarked, "Coleman is a murderer and will meet the same fate." At the court, Watters's mother pleaded with the judge to release her son, saying he was "a good boy but the dupe of others" and that she would ensure he was kept away from the "bad company" he had found himself in. The judge took a great interest in Watters's "bad company":

> Q. "Are you a member of the Irish Revolutionary Workers Party?"
> A. "I am."
> Q. "And you call yourself a Communist?"
> A. "I do."

It was all that the judge needed to hear: Watters was jailed for twelve months.[3]

The police were deployed across the city that morning in preparation for the demonstration. By late morning, thousands of people were coming out of their homes and meeting at the five designated gathering points for the demonstration: Canning Street in North Belfast, Templemore Avenue in East Belfast, Clonard Street on the Falls, Tennent Street on the Shankill, and Glengall Street in South Belfast. The plan was to march from these local districts and converge in a massive march on the Belfast workhouse where the Board of Guardians would be meeting. It did not take long to ascertain that the police intended to enforce the prohibition order on demonstrations—at each of the gathering points they had positioned themselves in such a way as to block the route of the march.

It was in East Belfast that the police acted first. At the Newtownards Road end of Templemore Avenue, a crowd had gathered with the intention of marching into the city center. Locals had temporarily commandeered the local library as a quasi-headquarters for planning and organizing the march. A large force of police and caged cars had gathered nearby, keeping the library under close watch. Shortly before 11:00 a.m. the crowd at Templemore Avenue had grown dense, but there was still no movement from the library. The police decided to move first: at around 11:30 a caged car pulled up outside the library, carrying a large group of police, who exited with batons at the ready. Three alleged leaders were arrested by police, though not without difficulty—a daring attempt was made to rescue them from the armored car as they were being taken away to police barracks.[4] In spite of this, the East Belfast marchers made a gallant effort to march through police lines, as reported by one journalist:

> In a few moments Templemore Avenue filled with men as if by magic from various side streets. They formed up in marching order, while at their head rushed a man wearing a cap shouting wildly, "Fall in and follow me." As the crowd continued to advance an order was given, "Draw batons—charge." Men in the crowd went down like nine-pins and the rest fled helter-skelter in the direction of the Albertbridge Road.[5]

James Kelly recalls that in addition to police efforts, other forces were at work to subdue East Belfast that day:

> From East Belfast there was a very different story. There the ODR workers were cowed by a local Unionist boss, a publican, who organised an Orange drummer to parade up and down Templemore Avenue beating a Lambeg drum as a warning to the shipyard workers to toe the line.[6]

There were attempts to reassemble at different points in the east of the city, and some stone-throwing occurred, but the baton charges had their effect, and the crowd dispersed, leaving the streets under police control. It was a similar story in North Belfast. There, the RUC had completely blocked the entrance to Canning Street, the designated assembly point, forcing people to gather in nearby Frederick Street. The police strategy of targeting known organizers was in full effect, and leading RWG organizer William Boyd was arrested immediately. With Boyd in custody the police turned their attention to the rest of the demonstrators, charging the crowd as they had done in East Belfast. In retaliation, protesters hurled a volley of stones, striking some of the police officers on the head, but it wasn't long until the police had the situation under control: within fifteen minutes Frederick Street had been cleared. The situation remained tense in the area for some time as crowds gathered in nearby streets. A journalist reported that one of the injured officers menacingly patrolled the streets in a police vehicle, peering out at those gathered, smiling as blood poured down his face.[7]

Perhaps owing to the treatment meted out by the police in the riots five days previously, demonstrators in South Belfast and Sandy Row were more reticent about confronting the forces of the state. A large crowd had gathered at Glengall Street, but the mere threat of violence from the police was enough to disperse those present. By lunchtime, it seemed like the police were gaining the upper hand. With the gatherings in the north, east, and south of the city effectively nullified, the police turned their attention to the west, where people had gathered on the Falls Road and on the Shankill.

As had happened in other districts, the police blocked the route of the march on the Falls Road. But there was a marked difference in the security operation in the Catholic neighborhood of the Falls, and it provided an early sign of the strategy the state would pursue in trying to suppress the movement. The police had shown up in far greater numbers there than they had elsewhere and were supported by considerable firepower. An ominous sight met those brave enough to make their way toward Clonard Street that morning. The police on duty on the Falls were armed with rifles and revolvers and were backed up by Whippet armored cars equipped with mounted machine guns. Despite being faced by the full might of the police force, some people attempted to break police lines: there was small-scale stone throwing and rioting on Balaclava Street, Albert Street, and Leeson Street throughout the morning. Unbeknownst to the people of the Falls, the police had no intention of confining themselves to baton use, and soon enough their revolvers were being drawn. On Leeson Street, the police opened fire on stone throwers, causing a stampede of people seeking cover from the hail of bullets emanating from police lines.

More and more police were rushed from other districts to the Falls. The orders they received were apparent to all who witnessed the events: as soon as police disembarked the caged cars they immediately opened fire. The RUC were firing wildly and indiscriminately: anyone who was on the street became a target. Sixteen-year-old Jon Davey, an auto mechanic, was wounded in the arm by a stray bullet that pierced the door of the garage he was working in. Thirty-three-year-old James Conlon from Bow Street was walking his young son from Milford Street School when he spotted police at the corner of street. Upon noticing that the police were aiming their rifles he sounded the alarm, shouting to two women standing nearby to take cover. The women and the boy escaped unharmed, but Conlon was shot in the leg, the bullet shattering his shinbone.[8] John Ramsey, a vegetable seller from Conway Street, was on his way home after finishing his rounds for the day when he was shot in the shoulder in Peel Street.[9] Not everyone escaped with their life: Samuel Baxter, a thirty-year-old flower-seller from Regent Street, was struck by a bullet on Cullingtree Road and died at the scene. It was thought that he wasn't even involved in the rioting but had been simply passing by the district when he was struck by a stray bullet. Local people did their best to help the wounded with the meager means at their disposal, described years later by an eyewitness:

> I saw a man being carried up to the Royal Hospital after he had been shot, some men held him by the legs and some by the arms. Cars were not plentiful in those days, so I suppose they were doing the only thing possible. I believe he died afterwards. I will never forget it, because young as I was, I thought the man must ·have been very poor by the clothes that he wore.[10]

Despite claims in the Unionist press that the police were "compelled to open fire" by stone throwers, there was no doubt that the police entered the Falls Road that day with the intention of violently repressing the march. This was evidence of a calculated policy on the part of the state aimed at dividing the movement. According to Paddy Devlin, Dawson Bates had sent instructions to the police to use guns on Catholic demonstrators but to confine themselves to only using batons in Protestant areas, his supposed reasoning being that it was necessary to prevent the IRA from using the demonstration to overthrow the government.[11] John Campbell, a guardian and secretary of the Northern Ireland Labour Party, was clear as to the motive of the state that day: "Lord Craigavon's solution was to divide the workers into different religious camps and it was noteworthy that although the recent trouble was spread all over the city only in Roman Catholic area did the police use their guns."[12]

Despite the onslaught of gunfire, the RUC faced fierce resistance from people in working-class districts along the Falls. The roads around Albert Street had recently been torn up for repairs so there was a ready-made assortment of materials for the rioters to use against the police. In the midst of the chaos, humor could still be found, recalled here by one republican activist: "I remember [an] incident; a fellow called Donald McNaughton, went and lifted a stone to throw at the cops, they fired and hit him on the hand, whereupon he fell. Immediately, he cried: *Don't tell the auld woman.* While others, taking his wound as serious, and thinking he was killed, called out: *Remember McNaughton*."[13] But with more and more police coming into the district it was clear that the Falls could not hold out. It was a pivotal moment: if the workers of the Falls were left isolated, the movement would be crushed and the door would be opened to attempts by the state to paint the movement as a Catholic and republican uprising.

The entire fate of the unemployed movement hung in the balance as people awaited the reaction of other areas to the attack on the Falls. On the Shankill, less than a mile away, thousands of people were still gathered, having been blocked by police from marching out of the area. There had been some small skirmishes with police throughout the morning, and the situation remained tense. Reporting that day from the Shankill were James Kelly and Mick Harkin of the *Irish Independent*. Immersing yourself in an illegal demonstration was beset with dangers in any case, but for two employees of a Dublin newspaper on the Protestant Shankill Road, it could be especially so. Harkin, the elder of the two, had just arrived in Belfast after a stint in New York and was anxious about the trip up the Shankill Road. It was a fear not shared by his colleague James Kelly, a talented twenty-one-year-old journalist with a desire to get in the thick of things. Despite his age, Kelly was no stranger to the dangers of sectarianism, having grown up nearby on the Falls Road. Unlike Harkin, Kelly had been witness to the changing mood of the working class in the preceding weeks and was confident that they would meet with little hostility. As they arrived on the Shankill, the two were far from incognito. Harkin, donned in a dapper tweed jacket and a dashing felt hat, stuck out like a sore thumb among the scruffy hordes of unemployed.

Fortunately, Harkin's fears were unfounded, as he and Kelly were welcomed with "open arms" when they declared that they were from the "Dublin papers." Kelly reported that the people of the Shankill seemed more concerned with the presence of the "ha'penny liar" of the Unionist *Belfast Telegraph* than the Nationalist press of the Free State. The two went about interviewing some of the thousands in attendance.[14] Gradually, whispers began to filter through the area that the Falls had come under attack. Kelly described the extraordinary scenes that followed:

On the Shankill Road crowds of growling men lounged around waiting. Suddenly a big red-faced woman with a black shawl thrown over her shoulders, wisps of hair hanging from her eyes appeared from nowhere. She shouted, "They are kicking the shite out of the peelers [police] up the Falls. Are you going to let them down." That seemed to be the flashpoint for the riot. These people started to burn a watchman's hut that had been used in an ODR scheme. The crowd dispersed in a panic when armed police came up in a cage car. Harkin and I—another reporter—took refuge in a shirt factory in Agnes Street and we saw some of the Protestant workers actually shooting at the police. . . . The police [retaliated]. They went about it in a workman-like fashion and there was no quarter given. That was a terrible afternoon on the Shankill. You could hear fire engines, shouts and roars, men crying, batons landing on skulls. It was a hell of a scene.[15]

The Shankill Road had erupted into a mass riot. "Fighting of the fiercest character raged through the Shankill for the entire day and there was scarcely an hour when the police were not in grips with crowds of men," the *Irish News* reported. "Charge after charge . . . had only a temporary effect upon them and they returned to the fray, always in increased numbers . . . This hide-and-seek affair continued throughout the day, on the Shankill Road were men and women shouting 'We must have bread' and other expressions and carrying sticks and stones and armed with pavers, dashed wildly from one street to another, pursued by the police."[16] Internal Communist documents report that the government attempts at divide and rule had failed:

In the storm areas of the religious rioting of former years there was a complete solidarity and interchange of speakers from the Protestant and Catholic areas. When actual fighting began it was undoubtedly heaviest in the Nationalist quarters. . . . But the Government were not successful in isolating the fighting to the Nationalist areas—Shankill Road Unionist area was made a centre of much [of the] fighting with the police and so also in the Ballymacarret area.[17]

It was clear that the police had lost control, and soon the rioting spread elsewhere. Within hours the entire city was gripped by upheaval, and the police were faced with a mass uprising of Belfast's workers. In a city long known for its deep sectarian divisions, the sight of working-class people confronting the state together was extraordinary—the *Irish News* summed up the mood of many when it said of the riots that "no more thrilling incidents in connection with the chequered history of Belfast have perhaps been witnessed."[18] The *Irish Independent* went even further, remarking that "Belfast is a city of ferment, almost a city of revolution."[19]

A carnival of rebellion ensued throughout the city. In York Street, people rushed a bread van, and a milk cart and coal cart were seized and their contents requisitioned. The people of North Belfast played their part too; their mass rioting ensued for many hours. In Ardoyne, buses and trams were overturned as "wild scenes" occurred in Old Park, where "for some time a battle royal took place as the men in blue were assailed from all sides, while women boohed and shouted."[20] The press was aghast at the fact that "even women took part in the terrific onslaught with stones and other missiles." Belfast Corporation property was a particular target of the rioters. Trams were hijacked and set alight. A Corporation bus was ransacked on the Crumlin Road. In fact, anything belonging to the Corporation was destroyed: sewer pipes, shovels, watchmen's huts, streets lamps, and lampposts were smashed or burnt. Tram and bus services were cancelled across the city. The response of the state to this uprising was vicious, described here by Robert Morrow, the secretary of the Belfast Trades Council:

> Never was such brutality used as was done in every district . . . no one was safe from the armed hooligans of police. . . . I don't believe that in [any other] place in the world could you have seen a greater display of armed force against the workers, armoured cars, cages [and] machine guns, everything that war stands for.[21]

In the intensity of the rioting, unusual alliances were being forged. There were reports that the B-Specials were active during the riots, but stories conflicted as to which side they were on. James Kelly reported that he witnessed Protestant men, who he was informed were off-duty Specials, firing on the RUC from a shirt factory in

Agnes Street. There were also reports that several B-Specials wearing civilian clothes (with the addition of a belt and a baton) were spotted assisting the police. When they appeared, a number of rioters recognized them as workers from the relief schemes and shouted "Wait till we get you on the job."[22] Possibly both of these stories are correct. The fact that the Orange State was viciously attacking Protestant people highlighted the contradictions within unionism. The B-Specials were a part-time police force, but many of their number were also part of Belfast's army of unemployed, and the riots sharply posed the contrast between these two positions. There were two choices: either stand by the state, or join fellow workers in rebelling against it. It was clear that the scale of the crisis was causing even the most ardent and loyal supporters of the Orange State to question or even discard their longstanding allegiances. It was even claimed that off-duty British soldiers were also involved in the rioting:

> An illustration of the height to which the mass struggle against the police developed is seen in the fact that two young soldiers, home on leave from the Royal Inniskilling Regt participated in the fight against the police, and were eventually arrested and given two months hard labour each. Young workers in the Royal Naval Volunteer Reserves also were charged for their activity.[23]

Local newspapers and politicians were also quick to claim IRA involvement in the riots. However, the overwhelming evidence appears to suggest that the IRA as an organization had very little to do with the ODR riots. Liam Mulholland, an IRA member in Ardoyne and a member of a local Unemployed Workers Committee, says that he had "about one hundred and fifty [IRA] men and I wasn't allowed to use those men [in the riots]."[24] Jack Brady, a staff officer with the IRA in Ballymacarrett, said that while they "had all the sympathy for the working class people" rioting, they "decided not to take part in anything like that" for fear that police intelligence "would take a photo or something and cry conspiracy."[25] It is possible that the IRA had underestimated the scale of the crisis in Belfast. Peadar O'Donnell, a member of the IRA Army Council at the time, remembers that after the unemployment riots in Britain he told the Officer Commanding of the IRA in Belfast: "'As sure as hell that'll spill over into Belfast.' But [the Officer Commanding] pooh-poohed the idea. But it did. And it caught the republican movement quite unprepared."[26] However, it was not only in Belfast that the republican movement refused to officially get involved in the unemployment agitation: they responded in similar fashion right across Ireland. When the RWGs organized a solidarity demonstration in Dublin, Seán Murray, who himself was an ex-IRA member and close to some leading elements in the group, wrote to the IRA asking that they participate in the rally. The brigade adjutant of the Dublin IRA replied and declined to participate in the demonstration: "I regret to inform you that owing to standing order, the Brigade as a Unit (Dublin Brigade), cannot parade at any meetings, demonstrations, etc, which are not under the direct control of the Army G.H.Q."[27]

It is clear therefore, that there was little official involvement from the IRA in the riots and that the republican movement did not see the importance of the unemployment question. However, many individual republicans were enthusiastically involved. Harry White, a legendary figure within republican folklore, remembered that the ODR riots "were the first political baptism of fire for a lot us," but "none of us were mobilised for the [riots], nor was the IRA behind it."[28] It is possible, however, that some IRA weapons were used to fire at the police: "Albert Price tells how Jimmy Ward was standing on top of a bin, firing with an old Martini rifle from Raglan Street. Every time he fired it, the recoil threw him off the bin. A big cheer would go up nonetheless."[29] However, another IRA member at the time, Seán Mac Con Uladh, suggests that the source of the weapons were unclear: "Anybody could have had guns in Belfast between 1922 and 1932."[30] Internal documents reveal that the RWGs, concerned to avoid the riots becoming being primarily focused on Nationalist areas, did make contact with the IRA during the riots and appear to have recruited some IRA members to the organization:

> On the commencement of the struggle the Secretariat [of the RWGs] got in touch with the leading elements of the IRA in Dublin. . . . The tactic of the Belfast capitalist class in its press, the

police etc was to make the Nationalist areas the centre of fighting. Our line was to see to it that action was not confined to the
Nationalist areas. With this the IRA were in agreement and as
a result of our meeting contact was established for the first time
with the Belfast IRA and the leadership of the Belfast [RWGs]
and some elements of the Belfast IRA have joined the groups.

The internal memo also suggests that individual IRA men coop-
erated with locals on the Shankill to launch attacks: "In the Shankill
according to a trustworthy report instances of the initiative in attacks on property [are] being taken by workers and some IRA men
thus bringing united action against the authorities."[31]

On top of the growing crisis in Belfast, there were fears that
the agitation could spread to Derry. On the evening of the first day
of the riots, a march was organized to the Derry Council, where a
deputation was granted access to the chambers. One man informed
the politicians that "there is a body of starving men outside, and
they want the Corporation's reply," while another, Mr. T. Donnelly,
warned the council "to see that the temper of the people was not dis-
turbed, or there might be havoc and destruction like Belfast." Before
leaving, one of those on the deputation, Mr. Brady, gave the council
an ultimatum, in an exchange with the mayor:

> Brady: What mandate are we carrying back to the unemployed?
> Mayor: That we will do our best according to our utmost means.
> Brady: And we will give you a week's time to do it.[32]

Dawson Bates imposed a curfew in Belfast in an effort to regain
control of the city: unauthorized persons were prohibited from walking the streets between the hours of 11:00 p.m. to 10:00 a.m. Once
again, however, the rioters got the better of the police. As evening
drew near, large numbers of men and women went out to the streets
and damaged the street lamps. As the sun began to set and darkness
began to fall, the dimly lit streets of Belfast became a shadowy no-
man's-land for the forces of the state and the police on patrol.

During the night, some five hundred police reinforcements
armed with rifles and bandoliers arrived in the city. They patrolled
with little effect and were seen scurrying through the streets un-

der a perpetual hail of stones and bricks emanating from unknown corners of the impenetrable darkness. There were also reports that the RUC had come under sniper attack, though no officers were wounded. It did not take long for the police to discover that in the blind conditions of night the advantage of being armed with rifles was rendered null.

On the Falls, the only flicker of light guiding the police came, ironically, from a simmering bonfire built out of watchmen's huts. According to one newspaper report, police cars were seen "dashing through the night, and military lorries carrying soldiers and quantities of barbed wire and other warlike equipment were seen going towards the east end of the city."[33] Searchlights were brought into the area, but the RUC command eventually decided that patrolling on foot was too dangerous. Unable to regain any semblance of control over the city, the RUC reduced themselves to amateurish attempts at stirring up sectarian tensions:

> Bands of RUC policemen, late at night, after the curfew, shouted in Catholic quarters: "Come out, you rebel bastards!," "Up King Billy!" etc. They were rewarded with a volley of kidney pavers. These "guardians of law and order" acting under orders of course, chalked up at Protestant quarters: "Sinn Féin is here," "To hell with the Boyne," and so on. This happened everywhere, but was of no avail.[34]

Local people made better use of the darkness than the police. Free from the revealing glare of the day, many men and women went into the streets, with pickaxes and shovels, to dig trenches and prepare barricades. They were actively preempting what was certain to be a vicious backlash by police the following day. The trenches and barricades would make travel by car through the streets impossible— meaning that police would have to leave their armored cars to enter the area. Groups of workers went out and tore up the streets—men were seen bringing down lampposts with sledgehammers and pickaxes in order to block the roads.

These efforts were not confined to one community, and extraordinary scenes of unity occurred in the interface areas, described by a journalist for the *Irish Independent*: "It is reported that men from the Falls Road and Shankill Road areas joined in digging trenches in the Kashmir Road district, between the Falls and the Shankill."[35] Even children played their part, helping to construct defenses against the RUC, recalled here by Eamon Ó Cianáin, who was eleven years old when he helped dig trenches from Lincoln Street on the Falls Road:

> The ODR rioters had their own songs that we used to sing as we dug up the paviours. Belfast streets were in the process of being concreted at that time. The corporation men were digging up the paviours street-by-street and laying down concrete. Lincoln Street had not been concreted when the riots started. We kids helped dig up the paviours to make the barricades so that the caged cars and the whippets of the R.U.C. could not come up the street.[36]

As dawn broke on the first day of rioting, the morning papers were full of reports from the "Battlezone" in Belfast, where the streets were indeed akin to those of a war-torn city. It was reported that a "noted Glasgow footballer"who was coming into town to sign for a local club took one look at the city as he was flying over and immediately got on the next plane home.[37] A report in the *Irish Independent*, probably written by James Kelly, vividly described the kinds of scenes that the Glasgow footballer would have witnessed when he arrived in Belfast:

> During the day I paid a visit to some of the "battle" areas. I saw some melancholy sights. Whole streets were a sea of churned-up soil, littered with cobblestones, bricks, sticks, broken bottles, and missiles of every description. Houses without a single whole pane of glass bore mute testimony to the fierceness of the struggles of the previous day.
>
> Here and there tired-eyed police, who, I was told, had been on continuous duty for 24 hours, directed civilians in the work of fill-ing in the deep trenches and removing the barricades of stones and timber. The men worked sullenly and unwillingly under the muz-zles of the police guns—they had been "commandeered" for the job.
>
> I penetrated into areas where, I was told, the police had not yet dared to show themselves and everywhere there was the same

tale of hungry and desperate people. "We cannot go on," they told me. "Jail is better than starvation."[38]

Despite the disastrous result of the police operation and their flagrant use of live fire, the Unionist press unreservedly defended the actions of the state. The police had been "compelled to open fire" by the rioters' actions, according to the *Belfast Telegraph*. The *Irish Independent* reported that "the trouble was not confined to any particular area of the city. It was equally intense in Ballymacarrett, Shankill Rd, Falls Rd and Ardoyne districts."[39] However, the Unionist press wished to ignore this and instead portray the riots as a Catholic and Communist uprising:

> Attempts have been made to exploit the discontent of the unemployed, and they have succeeded up to a point. . . . Communists and Bolshevists have been sowing the seed which in many cases under present conditions falls on fertile ground and produces a harvest usually of tears and sorrow . . . the misfortunes of the unemployed are of little moment to the Communist Party, which is out for the overthrow of Society. . . . By far the worst trouble was in quarters where the Northern Government is anathema, the forces of the Crown being subjected in the Falls area to attacks described by experienced policemen as the most persistent and violent they had ever seen. Most of the casualties and most of the arrests were in this area.[40]

While scornful of those that rioted, the Unionist press downplayed the riots in Protestant areas, with the *Telegraph* remarking that those rioting on the Shankill were mainly juvenile "fun-seekers." Thirty-four people were arrested during the riots and twenty men and three women were brought before the courts that morning. One of the defendants, Frederick Barr of Canton Street, had more reason than most for wishing to be released as soon as possible: "Can I get bail," he asked the judge, "as I have to fight Jack Flynn for the light-weight championship of Ireland tomorrow night."[41] Unfortunately, the judge did not look too kindly on the boxer's request, and all of the accused were denied bail and remanded in custody for eight days. Fred Barr's fight with Jack Flynn was cancelled and his involvement in the fight for Belfast's unemployed meant that he never got his shot at the title.

Despite everything that had happened, the Board of Guardians continued to demonstrate just how out of touch they were. As Belfast was in flames, the Guardians met to discuss how they should respond. The board seemed oblivious to events outside, with one member asking if "they realised the serious position whilst they were here, that the city was in a state of turmoil." It was proposed that the board should open up negotiations with the ODRWC, despite concerns about the role of Communists in the campaign. According to the board's meeting minutes, "[T]here was no use trying to avoid meeting certain people[.] It should be immaterial to the board whether it was a Bolshevist or a Communist. He certainly hoped also that they would not send one of these, but they should allow the men to nominate their own representative." The board, however, was still not prepared to begin negotiations, and the proposal fell by twenty votes to three.[42] The Guardians were still hoping to defeat the unemployed and issued a statement declaring that the strikers would be barred from relief if they did not resume work, a move described by one Guardian as an attempt to "break the strike."[43]

The police had their own plans to break the strike. Throughout the night they had been preparing to reclaim control over the working-class districts of Belfast. In preparation for the day's events, the police concentrated large deployments of caged cars as well as civilian vehicles such as lorries in the city. While foot patrols were deemed too dangerous, travelling by car came with its own difficulties, according to one newspaper report: "The barricades were two feet high in places, and consisted of stones which had been dug up. Trenches were also dug in the streets and in certain areas there were as many as three barricades in a row at intervals of about twenty yards. . . . Moreover, the toll on the tyres was heavy, as bottles had been smashed freely."[44]

With the Royal Inniskilling Fusiliers at Hollywood Barracks placed on standby in case the police should fail, the operation to reclaim the Falls commenced at around 8:00 a.m. on Wednesday morning, October 12. Police appeared in force and smashed their way through the barricades. House by house, they broke down doors and made wholesale arrests. The Belfast press, including the *Northern Whig*, claimed that the police were seeking "armed communist agitators," "IRA gunmen," and "secret documents" that would prove the existence of an organized conspiracy.[45]

Those who were not remanded into custody were dragged out of their beds and forced at bayonet point into the streets and told to dismantle the barricades. The RUC were not picky about who they dragged out of bed: among those forced to remove the barricades were four blind people. The *Belfast Telegraph* gloated that "it was an interesting spectacle to see the civilian population engaged in an occupation which apparently was not much to their liking."[46] Ironically, one of those ordered outside by the police was in fact a Nationalist member of the Board of Guardians:

> Mr. James Collins, a Poor Law Guardian, residing in Quinn St, alleges he was taken out of his bed by about a dozen policemen last night, and, during a downpour of rain, when clothed only in an overcoat, and pyjamas and assisted by his 16-year-old son, made to remove a barricade. His wife and his family, he declares, are living in terror and abandoning their home tonight.[47]

Police also attempted to stop food supplies from entering the Falls in an effort to break the resistance in the district. They were met by hundreds of mainly female mill workers, many in their bare feet, who helped break police cordons so as to allow food supplies into the area. The women workers from the mills played a very important part in resisting the police. They had been one of the only sectors to have heeded the call for a general strike, and many of them were on the front lines of the rioting. Bob Bradshaw, a twenty-year-old IRA member, remembers that he was "up to his neck in [the riots], throwing pickers (paving stones) at the police," when "two B. Specials grabbed him, drawing back the well greased firing pin of his rifle." Bob believed it was "the end" for him, however, "at that moment, a horde of mill girls flocked in front of him and the danger was averted."[48]

Despite the ferocity of their onslaught, the police were unable to regain control of the Falls or the rest of the city, and Belfast was gripped by rioting for a second day. There were more trenches dug, more shots fired, and more people injured. Though no one else was killed, forty-year-old Leeson Street resident John Keenan, who had been seriously injured by a gunshot wound the previous day, died of his injuries. Disgracefully, Keenan's wife, Mary, was refused compensation for his murder after the riots, the judge ruling that "strictly speaking, he had no proof Keenan was killed by a bullet wound."[49] All in all, two people had been shot dead by the RUC, and another fifteen suffered gunshot wounds, including two who were shot in the back.[50]

By Wednesday evening, after two full days of rioting, the situation in Belfast had become so grave that the prime minister of Northern Ireland, Lord Craigavon, released a personal appeal to the Protestant workers and unemployed of Belfast to remain loyal to the state:

> I want to make a very earnest appeal to our people who have stood aloof from the Board of Guardians during the past week to come forward. If they will go back to work, if they will cease to take the "advice" of outsiders, if they will act like Ulstermen have always done and go back to work, then I will personally see that all these schemes are hurried on. . . . I will urge my friends, private and personal, to come forward and prevent the labouring classes from cutting off their noses to spite their face.

Craigavon had stern words for those who would defy him:

> Just one word, and one word only . . . to those mischief makers who have come into our midst. If they have designs by the trouble which they have brought into our city, if they have the idea at the back of their minds that this is one way of securing a Republic for all of Ireland . . . then I say with you ladies and gentlemen—Never . . . and I will add that I am not a man to be intimidated.[51]

Despite Craigavon's defiance, his government was scrambling behind the scenes to work out a deal and was "determined to end the strike by foul means or fair."[52] Sections of the Unionist establishment were becoming increasingly worried, demanding that the government do something to appease the unemployed. Seventeen councillors, including ten from the Unionist Party, signed a motion calling on the government "to take such action as may be necessary to relieve distress and starvation amongst the unemployed people of the city."[53] The last straw came on Wednesday evening at the Belfast Trades Council meeting in the ILP hall. After weeks of procrastinating, the city's union leaders agreed that the Trades Council would call for a general strike if the ODR workers' demands were not met.

That evening the Guardians were called to a meeting with cabinet ministers and were told in no uncertain terms that they were to come up with new rates of relief. Privately, Craigavon reasoned that an acceptance of the strikers' demands was likely to prove less costly than allowing the riots to continue. According to Sir Wilfrid Spender, head of the Northern Ireland Civil Service, "The agitation had got so serious that he believed that they might have found themselves confronted with willful damage which would be out of all proportion to the [money] paid away on Relief schemes."[54]

While Craigavon and the Unionist Party were clamoring to end the dispute, the RWGs were working diligently to continue the agitation and broaden their base of support. It was an opportune time: the group had never had a higher profile, and their role in leading the movement was widely acknowledged and respected in working-class areas. Still more, the actions of the state during the riots that week had raised questions among Protestant working-class people about the Unionist Party, opening up the possibility of building a movement in areas like the Shankill that could challenge the hold of the Orange State. This opening existed in both Protestant and Catholic areas, and the cross-community resistance seen during the riot offered a rare but concrete example of the possibilities for working-class unity over sectarianism. Before the rise of unemployment agitation, the RWG leadership had seen itself as a provisional organization that would prepare for the launch of a mass Communist Party at some future date when circumstances were more favorable. But now, with a militant cross-community resistance taking shape before their eyes, the RWGs considered that the moment had arrived. In response to Craigavon's sectarian appeal, the RWGs released their own statement, likely written by Tommy Geehan and addressed to all the workers of Belfast. The statement was posted across the city:

> Fellow workers: In this city two forces stand clearly opposed to one another; the high priests of hunger, the watchdogs of wealth and property at the head of the Guardians, the Municipal Council and the local Government on the one side, and the workmen of the city, their wives and families on the other. The Relief workers' fight is the battle of the whole working class. A new era is opening in the Irish working class movement. . . . The future is plainly one of stormy class battle.
>
> The policy of the Unionist Party, the servants of big finance and industry? This policy has been a disaster for the Northern workers[.] The policy of Mr. Devlin and the Nationalists? This party can only serve the interests of the conservative imperialists by standing in the way of the united class struggle of workers. . . . Reformist Labour? [Their] policy . . . is strangling the trade union movement, holding back the organised workers. . . . And the alternative? The development of a strong united working class movement built directly from the ranks of the toilers in the mills and factories, on the docks and railways, Labour exchanges and Relief jobs, in all work places.
>
> The workers organised in the Revolutionary Workers' Groups—the Communists—are working for the building of such a movement of the Irish working-class[.] To the task men and women of the working-class of Belfast and all Ireland. Not through the Tory imperialism of Craigavon can the Northern workers escape from miserable wages, idleness and the Poor-Law, not through the National Reformism of De Valera can a free Ireland be achieved. [Only through] the creation of a powerful All-Ireland Workers' Party—the Communist Party of Ireland—can the starvation policy of the capitalists be defeated, their rule and that of imperialism over Ireland be broken, and a united independent nation, a workers' and farmers' Republic be brought into being.[55]

There were certainly grounds for hoping that the RWGs could expand and recruit rapidly, but they would have to do so in the face of an organized anticommunist backlash emerging in Belfast. Three RWG members were arrested,[56] and rumours were spread that police patrols were on the hunt for Tommy Geehan, who had so far avoided capture and "seemed to enjoy a charmed life."[57] Geehan's evasion of the authorities, however, was more than simple luck: "Tommy Geehan, for a time was in hiding; the police wanted him," remembered RWG member Betty Sinclair. "This involved moving him from one place to another. [We] succeeded in saving Tommy Geehan from arrest."[58]

The press campaign against the RWGs was now in full swing, and newspaper reports blamed the violence during the riots on "outside agitators with orders and money from Moscow." The Russian theme was furthered by the *Daily Mail*, which reported a "husky Russian" agitating among the rioters, while the *Telegraph* matter-of-factly stated that the "activities of the Communist Party prove conclusively that they were at the bottom of the outbreak":

> Some facts stand out prominently which give much food for thought. The first of these is the excellent organisation which prevailed amongst the rioters of Tuesday. It was no overboiling of temper at being refused permission to march to the workhouse. That was but the camouflage of the opportunity to make trouble. . . . The leaders have been in touch with the socialist extremists across the water for some time past . . . and for some days before the trouble developed some of these succeeded in entering Northern Ireland.[59]

Although the RWGs had played an important role in initiating and leading the unemployment movement, there was no truth to the claim that they were coordinating the riots. Although they were by no means pacifist, the RWGs had focused on building a mass movement of unemployed rather than orchestrating violent confrontations. Throughout the previous months, they had urged their supporters to avoid riots with the police, and all the evidence suggests that they had planned for a peaceful demonstration that Tuesday. Given the state ban, however, and the provocative behavior of the RUC, resistance was inevitable, and the RWGs unequivocally defended their supporters' actions. There is a considerable difference between offering political and moral support to rioters and actively coordinating them. In fact, it was claimed that much of the leadership of the RWGs was not even present during the rioting, having gone into hiding knowing that the police had plans to arrest them on sight.[60] The truth is that even if the RWGs had wanted to, they were far too small to organize something on the scale of the resistance in Belfast. The riots were not the result of a conspiracy on the part of a small group of Communists; they were the organic expression of deep anger building up inside of thousands of people, the conscious resistance of a class that would take no more.

Unfortunately, the backlash against the RWGs was more extensive than these accusations. Both the Catholic Church and various denominations within Protestantism used the pulpit to denounce what was commonly dubbed the "red menace." On the first day of the riot, at the autumn meeting of Catholic bishops in Maynooth, Cardinal MacRory explained that more priests would need to be recruited to assist in the war against Communism. In the strongest possible terms he told those gathered that Communists were the "anti-Christ" and that the spread of Bolshevism in Ireland was "the great apostasy which the apostle said would presage the end of the world."[61] The red-baiting was equally fierce on the Protestant side: on the Sunday after the riots, Rev. John McCaffrey delivered a sermon at the Shankill Road Methodist Church entitled "Has the Shankill Road Turned Its Back on the Bible?," warning his parishioners that it was their biblical duty to remain loyal to the Unionist state and urging that they repent for the "mad outburst of Bolshevism, Godlessness and downright wickedness" that had been seen on the road in the days previous:

> The deplorable scenes and acts of lawlessness committed in the city and particularly those committed on this Road and in the adjoining streets humiliate us all . . . there is a lowering of the prestige of our city and Province . . . brought about through the insidious and irrational propaganda of Communistic intriguers.
>
> You and I are located in a section of this city which for a very long time has been a stronghold of the Orange Institution[.] That institution laid upon me two solemn obligations: 1—regard for the Bible as the rule of my belief and conduct and 2—loyalty to the state and to constitutional law—loyalty which prohibits any truck with traitors or enemies of the state.[62]

As debate about the threat of communism and the implications of the riots raged through the city, powerful forces were at work behind the scenes to bring the crisis to an end. By Friday, much of the rioting had subsided, but the barricades were still up, and the police had failed to regain complete control of the city. With the state of the city still in flux and the threat of a general strike on the horizon, the Unionist government finally "found" the money to offer the unemployed a deal. The Board of Guardians, which had pleaded poverty throughout the campaign, now offered new rates of relief—thirty-two shillings a week for a couple with five children or more, twenty-eight shillings a week for a couple with three or four children, twenty-four shillings a week for a couple with one or two children, and twenty shillings a week for a couple with no children. Besides effectively doubling the rate of relief, other demands of the strikers were also met: relief would no longer be paid in kind but in cash, and the means test would be modified. Against the Guardians' express wishes, it was announced that those who had been suspended during the strike would be kept on relief. There was one important omission: the demand that single people be paid relief was not offered. The strikers agreed to meet in St. Mary's Hall to discuss the proposal on Saturday night.

Before the offer was put to a vote, the unemployed of Belfast had one more pressing engagement. On Friday morning, the coffins of the two men killed during the riots, Samuel Baxter and John Keenan, were paraded in somber splendor through the streets of Belfast, followed by a vast sea of supporters. Despite a biting autumn wind, which "pierced through thin and frayed coats," around one hundred thousand people came out to greet the cortege in "an extraordinary demonstration of sympathy" to pay their respects to the Catholic man and the Protestant man who were slain by Lord Craigavon's military police.[63] In a testament to the esteem in which the RWGs were held, some of their members, including Betty Sinclair and Lily Magill, were chosen to be pallbearers at the funeral. Another pallbearer was Tom Mann, the veteran British Communist and organizer of the unemployed, who had arrived to speak at a meeting organized by the RWGs the following day. At the gates of the cemetery, police swooped in on Mann. He describes what happened to him that day:

> I arrived in Belfast at 6.30 a.m. on Friday morning, Oct. 14th and my first surprise was to see 500 soldiers disembarking and lining up for marching. I had the attention of the [police] from the first jump off the boat; they didn't interfere with me in any way during the morning beyond that of following me wherever I went. I joined in the great funeral procession of Comrade Baxter in the afternoon, the other comrade having been buried during the morning. I was by the coffin the whole 2 and half hours—the time it took to march through the city, while hundreds of thousands lined the sidewalks to the gates of the cemetery. I reached the gates of the cemetery; a police detective touched me on the shoulder and said sharply, "You'll come along with us, Mr. Mann."[64]

The arrest of Tom Mann showed just how paranoid the establishment was about the involvement of Communists in the unrest, a fear epitomized by the suggestion in the Unionist press that the seventy-five-year-old Mann had been called into Belfast to organize a general strike. In a farcical turn, the police told Mann that he was to be deported, but it turned out there was no provision for this under existing law, as Mann was a British citizen. Instead, he was presented with an exclusion order from everywhere in Northern Ireland except Clogher in Tyrone, and as a result he got the first boat back to Liverpool. Mann was good-humoured about his deportation, proudly telling reporters, "One more for the collection . . . Altogether I have been deported from about five countries."[65]

As Tom Mann was pondering a life in exile from Clogher, the striking ODR workers gathered in St. Mary's Hall to discuss the offer from the Guardians. They had been there many times before in the last week and half, but there was little doubting that this was the most substantial offer they had yet received, perhaps the best they would get. The room was packed to the rafters, and, as usual, the chair of the ODRWC opened proceedings, according to the *Irish Workers' Voice*:

> Tommy Geehan rose to his feet. The cheering swelled to a roar; the stamping feet seemed like thunder. At last it died down. "Com-

rades," began Tommy, "I want to say at the outset that we have won a glorious victory." His voice was drowned in the exultant shouts. On every face you could see stamped the consciousness of having won a great class triumph.

"We have achieved a glorious victory," said Geehan. "It is a direct contradiction to all who said that the workers could not be united and would not fight. The last two weeks would be recorded as two of the most glorious in the history of the working class in Belfast. First of all, they saw Protestant and Catholic workers marching together, and on Tuesday they saw them fighting together."[66]

Geehan then proposed that the offer be accepted, and he was seconded by Henry Finlay of the Shankill Road. Not everyone was pleased with the deal: single men still felt aggrieved at being left out of the offer. While the deal stipulated they would now be entitled to benefits, most did not qualify. It was a difficult situation for the RWGs: there were solid grounds for claiming that the offer was the best the unemployed could hope to achieve—the street riots could not go on forever, and eventually the greater firepower of the police would give them the upper hand. There was, of course, the threat of the general strike, which could have forced more from the state, but the labor leaders had proven unwilling to support such an action in the past and there was no guarantee that they would deliver this time around. The RWGs found themselves in a delicate situation. The decision to support the offer came with consequences—the mostly young, single men who had little reason to endorse the offer had been some of the most militant participants in the movement. It was they who had entered the workhouse, who had blocked the roads to stop the exit of the Guardians, and who had done much of the street fighting and therefore borne the brunt of the police violence. On balance, the RWGs took the decision they thought was best, but in doing so they isolated themselves from some of their most ardent followers and potential recruits.

Nevertheless, it was the strikers and not the RWGs who ultimately voted on the offer at the meeting. The motion to accept the offer was put to a vote and a clear majority of the nearly two thousand workers in the room supported it, with only around fifty voting against. The mood in the hall was ecstatic, and a strong sense of optimism prevailed. One worker from Ballymacarrett declared that "bluff and flag waving would never work again." He added that not only was the working class in Belfast united, the "workers of Dublin and the South and England were behind them" too.[67] A small token of this solidarity could be seen in Worksop in England that day, where women, leading one of a series of hunger marches held that year, on their way to London passed a resolution congratulating the workers of Belfast in their successful fight for the unemployed and "condemning the action of the Government in using troops to shoot down workers in their struggle for bread."[68]

Fittingly, Tommy Geehan, who had played such a crucial role in the movement, closed the meeting, with typical gusto:

> When the history of the working class [is] written, the past two weeks [will] stand out as a glorious record of Protestant and Roman Catholic workers marching shoulder to shoulder and fighting together. Never in history did the working class achieve anything without mass struggle and sacrifice.... [T]he victory of the Relief workers brought a little ray of hope into many working class homes, but [we] will struggle on until every man, woman and child [is] living in peace and prosperity and happiness.[69]

The great strike of the ODR workers was over. Despite the unchanged predicament of the single unemployed, most people across the city saw it as a tremendous victory, and there was jubilation in the working-class districts of Belfast. By Monday, the ODR workers were back at work, and by Tuesday the curfew was lifted. Belfast returned to some semblance of normality, though the strike's reverberations would be felt for some time to come. In just three months, a small group of revolutionaries had built a mass movement that brought Belfast to a standstill, shaking the Unionist establishment to its core. It was an incredible achievement which, if nothing else, discredited the assumption that Catholics and Protestants would never unite, and left future generations with a shining example of workers' unity, indelibly etched in the annals of Belfast's troubled history.

Chapter 6

AFTERMATH:
CLASS, SECTARIANISM, AND THE LEFT

The riots of October 1932 presented the very real possibility for the emergence of a rejuvenated and empowered working-class movement in Northern Ireland. The RWGs—whose profile had skyrocketed owing to their role in the ODR struggle—now had an opportunity to build the kind of Communist Party that had been formed in most other European countries but had hitherto failed to develop in Ireland. The Communists were immensely optimistic about the prospects for building such an organization, assured that the bankruptcy of reformism and the superiority of revolutionary leadership had been proven in the course of the struggle. The ODR strike was, for the RWGs, a prelude to a "revolutionary situation," where the last vestiges of sectarianism had been effectively wiped out in the process of common struggle.

Unfortunately, this perspective was premature on both counts: the post-October terrain showed neither an absolute escalation in workers' militancy nor a terminal decline in sectarianism. This is not to say that the unity on display in 1932 was an isolated incident: significant periods of working-class struggle continued in the years that followed, and both the reformist and revolutionary Left experienced growth in membership. But powerful forces were at work to counteract this through the rekindling of sectarian divisions. It was the struggle between these two countervailing tendencies—class politics and sectarianism—and the balances of forces that each of these tendencies could realize that would ultimately prove crucial in determining the trajectory of working-class politics in the 1930s.

It did not take long after the riots to realize that Belfast was not on the verge of a socialist revolution. While the ODR strike had been a significant event, it was far from a pre-revolutionary situation. For one, despite their impressive recent successes, the Communists themselves were far too small an organization and were in no position to be leading a revolution, something they must have realized themselves. Furthermore, the unemployed union which they led, while much bigger than the RWGs, still only represented a few thousand workers, leaving the thousands of people who had taken part in the riots and protests still largely unorganized.

This level of disorganization on the Left was compounded by a mechanical insistence on the part of the RWGs that all sectarian prejudices had been eliminated during the course of the strike. While the ODR riots had posed a forceful challenge to reactionary ideas in the heads of workers, this did not automatically translate into a consistent anti-sectarian consciousness. Undoubtedly, a minority of workers on both sides had drawn anti-sectarian conclusions from the riots, and indeed some joined the RWGs. But in order to break the mass of workers from sectarian ideas a much more protracted struggle was needed, combined with a conscious ideological challenge on the part of the RWGs against both sectarianism and the organizations that propagated it within the working class. As the socialist historian Mike Milotte puts it:

> The fact that some unemployed Protestants were fighting the police did not . . . mean that they, let alone the Protestant working class as a whole, or even all the Catholics who participated in the struggle, were fighting for a united Ireland or for socialism. Such a spontaneous emergence of proletarian anti-imperialist consciousness could not simply be assumed[.] That did not mean, of course, that an event as traumatic as the October upheaval was irrelevant to the overcoming of sectarian and political divisions within the working class. The problem was one of political leadership and political organisation[,] for which the incantation of revolutionary slogans was no substitute.[1]

The RWGs were favorably placed to join the struggle over economic issues with a wider ideological battle against sectarianism. Unlike the broad labor movement and the rest of the Left, the RWGs maintained a principled stance against sectarianism. However, the Communists exhibited a mechanical understanding of how the basic economic issues and the more complicated political challenges were interlinked, and how religious divisions might be exposed and directly challenged in the course of winning the Outdoor Relief campaign. They displayed an overly optimistic faith that campaigning over bread-and-butter issues would be sufficient to overcome sectarianism in the wider movement, as if a period of intensive common struggle would be sufficient to dislodge more than a century of sectarian indoctrination. In the whirlwind of activity that accompanied the unemployed struggles, the Communists downplayed the importance of winning their membership and their substantial cross-community support base to a consistent ideological opposition to sectarianism.

These shortcomings were greatly exacerbated by the exaggerated political perspective of the RWGs. Like the Communist movement internationally, RWG activists in Belfast were guided by the Comintern in Moscow, which insisted that the world was on an inexorable trajectory toward revolution. Given this perspective, it was assumed that building a broad base of support among the working class was not necessary for Communist agitation, since a small group of revolutionaries could galvanize the already-revolutionary masses. Such a perspective did not itself pose an obstacle to deepening class unity in Belfast in the short term. This was combined, however, with an extremely divisive approach toward the rest of the labor movement, informed by the Stalinist notion that all shades of reformism were a variant of "social-fascism," to be treated with the same disdain as the parties of the Far Right. For Communists in the North, as in many other places around the globe, this was a recipe for isolation and disaster, and they would find themselves in difficulty very quickly.

In the early stages of the unemployed movement, most reformist forces in Belfast—including the leadership of the trade unions and the NILP—had abandoned the field of struggle. For this reason, the

RWGs were able to build a movement without having to relate to them. However, as the campaign developed and wider forces became involved, the "class against class" strategy inherited from the Comintern became a hindrance. By completely rejecting any alliances with reformist forces, the RWGs isolated themselves from the broad membership of the trade union movement and from the leftward-moving rank and file of the NILP, depriving them of the audience needed to form the mass party they wished to create. By November 1932, the RWGs had 120 members in Belfast (up from around 30 the year previously) and 6 members in Coleraine. The total national membership was 339. Additionally the RWG paper now had a circulation of three thousand, with fifteen hundred of those sold in Belfast (an increase from a total circulation of 360 the previous July).[2] A Young Communist League (YCL) was also formed in the city to recruit young workers. Twenty-four people joined the group in Belfast, with internal documents suggesting that the "majority of the [YCL members] come from the unionist Protestant areas."[3] This growth was moderately impressive and indicative of the growing influence of the RWGs, but it fell far short of the critical mass they required to launch a mass party.

One tragic consequence of the gap between the RWG's modest influence and their divisive posturing was their inability to hold together a united unemployed movement as splits began to emerge. The first fissure came within weeks of the ODR riots, when left-wing members of the NILP, angry at the RWG's decision to call off the strike, formed an organization for the single unemployed. The RWGs bitterly opposed this move, but the new group grew quickly, claiming a membership of five hundred within a few weeks. The divisions within the movement were not lost on paid defenders of the Unionist state either, who were keen to see the back of a united working class. Correspondence between the RUC and the Ministry of Home Affairs reveals that they thought that the split was "to the good" of the situation and hoped that the new group would "cut out the communist element as far as possible."[4] The movement was further divided in November 1932 when the Trades Council launched its own moderate organization of the unemployed. The unemployed were now split three ways. Despite this, the campaign backed by the RWGs was by the far the most influential, and meetings still attracted hundreds, sometimes even thousands of people months after the ODR riots and well into 1933. Nevertheless, the increasing fragmentation was a bitter blow to the project.

The Communists still had considerable influence within the working class, for all of their divisive politics. Tommy Geehan was their best-known figure, and had developed the nickname "Molotov," presumably after the crude Russian incendiary device. The RWGs stood him in the 1933 election for the Board of Guardians, in the Court Ward—a mainly Protestant constituency that included much of the Shankill Road—where he polled more than twelve hundred votes on a limited franchise but failed to get elected. Much was made in the press and at the pulpit about Geehan's Marxist politics. At a mass meeting of the unemployed held on October 26, 1932, he told those assembled "that he came into the fight as a Communist and would go out as one."[5] Here Geehan wasn't simply declaring his political affiliation; he was responding to the anticommunist offensive that was being launched across Belfast and Ireland in general. Just days after the end of the ODR dispute, for example, the Youth Evangelistic Campaign brought twenty preachers to Belfast for a three-week mission against communism.[6]

Despite the problems faced by the unemployment movement and the strategic limitations of the RWGs, there were signs that the unity that had been built during the ODR campaign was far from dead. This was exemplified by the extraordinary dispute between Great Northern Railway (GNR) workers and their bosses in 1933, an intense confrontation between a mainly Protestant workforce and railway companies that would become one of the most violent in the history of Ireland. In November 1932, the Irish railway companies applied to the Railway Wages Board for a cut in wages for their staff, resulting in a 10 percent reduction in pay. The trade unions representing the workers rejected this cut, and on January 31, 1933, railwaymen employed in five of the six rail companies operating in the North voted to begin strike action. Unlike the ODR strike, the action had the support of the official unions—in this case the Associated Society of Locomotive Engineers and Firemen and the National Union of Railwaymen—who feared that the wage cuts were the beginning of a wider assault on workers in other industries.

The *Belfast Telegraph* reported that up to six thousand workers from four different systems were involved in the stoppage. Workers on the Free State end of the GNR railway line "also threw in their lot with the strikers, and turned out in full strength." As the strike began, chaos and confusion paralyzed the system, resulting in a near-complete shutdown of rail traffic. There were also signs that this was no normal stoppage. Viral wires at Balmoral signal cabin were cut, and the GNR telegraph and telephone lines were severed, which according to the *Belfast Telegraph*, temporarily "crippled communications":

> Great Victoria Station itself was a centre of gloom. The dull morning, coupled with fog, added to the depression and the carriage windows lacked the spotless brightness that has come to be associated with the system. Even the engines seemed to resent strange hands—at any rate they were dirty and failed to give the impression of life and power. . . . Officials were hurrying up and down the platform making arrangements and passed the silent groups of strikers with never a word. Gone was all the camaraderie of old, and the presence of detectives and police who kept passing up and down the trains was further evidence of the grimness of the situation.[7]

Rail stations in Derry, Clones, Omagh, Ballymena, Ballymoney, Cookstown, Coleraine, Portrush, Strabane, Enniskillen, Newry, Lurgan, Whitehead, and Carrickfergus were all closed. Over a hundred workers came out in Dundalk. Dublin was deserted. The strike united both North and South. The Unionist government, however, was again prepared to resist this example of united working-class action. Indeed, some government ministers were railway company directors themselves; Minister for Home Affairs Dawson Bates had his own train to bring him from Portrush to Belfast every morning.

Abetted by the Unionist government, the railway owners set out to break the strike. Trucks and buses were commandeered to move goods, and strikebreakers known as "blacklegs" were employed throughout the industry to keep the trains going. The scabs were drawn mainly from railway management and from the Queen's University student body, and were paid twice the normal rate for a rail worker. The students were treated especially well for their service: special provisions were made for them at a local hotel, and detectives were put in place to guarantee their protection.[8] The use of students as strikebreakers received widespread condemnation. NILP politician Harry Midgley moved a motion that the Belfast Corporation should rescind the £7000 per annum that the Corporation gave Queen's University in grants and remission of rates because of its role in the strike. Other students at Queen's were also critical of the scabs: the University's Literary and Scientific Society passed a resolution condemning students for involving themselves in "a purely private dispute between railway companies and their employees."[9]

The strikers did not take the use of scabs lightly, however, and many of the pickets grew increasingly violent. On the second day of the strike, a train carrying mail left Dublin rail station at 9:00 a.m. bound for Belfast. At around 10:15 a.m. the train was negotiating a bend two hundred yards from the level crossing at Dromiskin and some seven miles south of Dundalk. Suddenly the train lurched to one side and then to the other before finally derailing and crashing down an embankment twenty feet below. The train was completely destroyed. Robert Patterson, who was sitting in the mail van when the crash occurred, died at the scene. Another man, John McWilliams, died later in the County Infirmary in Dundalk.[10]

The trade unions forcefully denied any responsibility for the derailment, and it is highly likely that the train crash was the result of sabotage by strikers or supporters, even if it was unsanctioned by union officials. Prior to the fatal accident another train had been stopped in Dundalk, whereupon a number of men entered and removed the driver.[11] An official investigation found that "no doubt a rail was removed from each of the lines," leading to the crash.[12] Indeed, one newspaper claimed that the RWGs distributed a leaflet to strikers that said, "No tears for the fate of the 'blacklegs'; the railway bosses are responsible for every life endangered in strike-breaking activities."[13]

Both sides in this dispute understood the wider significance of the strike. The Unionist government—in alliance with its counterparts in the Irish Free State—intensified its intervention into the strike, as reported here by a journalist:

> An unexpected development took place, when several lorry loads of armed soldiers arrived in Dundalk from Dublin with armoured cars and mounted machine-guns. The soldiers, wearing tin hats, were conveyed in lorries through the town and along the roads over which buses were operating, patrolling the roads to prevent obstruction by the felling of trees.[14]

Armored RUC cars escorted lorries driven by blacklegs in the North while the Gardaí (the police force in the Irish Free State) and the Irish Army escorted buses in the South. The level of solidarity with the strike was considerable, and the stoning of railway lorries and buses became common even in the remotest of towns. Violence intensified as the strike continued. The RUC had stepped up their security operation, and a one-hundred-strong flying squad armed with rifles patrolled the Belfast Railway lines. The unions responded by spreading the strike. Bus workers in the South of Ireland who worked for the GNR were brought out on strike, spreading the dispute to sections of the Irish Free State. When a GNR bus driven by a scab reached Dublin it was hijacked and set alight, causing a full-scale riot when the Gardaí arrived to baton-charge the crowds.[15] It was even reported that scabs were sleeping in special quarters in Dundalk under the armed protection of the Free State armed forces.[16]

The violence at times was intense: strikers with stones would ambush buses and trains and the drivers of railway lorries were threatened if they did not respect the picket line. On Saturday, March 26, a bomb was thrown at a bus in York Road, rebounding and exploding on the streets. Five men were hurt. Sabotage surrounding the strike continued to grow. An attempt was made to blow up a bridge above the railway line in Dunmurry in Belfast. Although the blast "shook houses in Dunmurry and was heard more than two miles away," the charge had not been not properly set, and the bridge structure remained intact.[17] On Saturday, February 25, bombs were thrown at railway stations in Whitla Street and another from Boyne Bridge in Belfast.[18] Those continuing to work on the railway lines could also be targeted. Robert Ewing, a railway worker from Letterkenny, was abducted by two men as he cycled home from work. The abductors, who spoke largely in Gaelic, told Ewing that they intended to interrogate him at an unknown location in Donegal. The plan, however, was foiled, and the railway worker was released.

The increasing level of violence surrounding the strike suggested significant coordination, and indeed there was. Bob Bradshaw, an IRA member at the time, remembers how republicans became involved:

> Davey Matthews, our O/C [Officer Commanding], was approached one night, sitting by his kitchen fire when two Protestant men knocked. "Our men are hard pressed," they complained. "The Great Northern are still running trains and they are also managing to deliver goods by lorry. Now if the IRA would stop them, they might be prepared to settle." . . . "The only way we could stop them," said Matthews, "would be by blowing up the railway." "We thought of that," the Protestant workers told him, "but we had no one that could do it."[19]

On February 28, an IRA unit fired shots at scab truck drivers just off the Falls Road. They were chased by an RUC unit but escaped and shot one RUC man, later named as John Ryan from Tipperary, who died from his wounds. This was not the end of IRA involvement, and throughout the strike they continued to intervene by setting off bombs under bridges and throwing grenades at railway property. The joint involvement of republicans and Communists had greatly alarmed the Unionist government, with Northern Ireland prime minister James Craig describing it as an "insidious attempt by Nationalists, Communists, and Socialists to betray Ulster into an all-Ireland Republic."[20]

The RWGs were also involved in both the strike and solidarity work. One of their members, William Crozier, was the chair of an unofficial Belfast strike committee, which organized much of the militant action carried out by the strikers. They also used their Relief Workers Committee to build resistance to the use of unemployed workers as strikebreakers. The RWGs were insistent that the strike should be led by its rank and file and were highly suspicious of trade

union officials. Indeed, Tommy Geehan compared the "respectability of the present railway strike, and the difference between it and the
ODR struggle."[21] He believed that the struggle had "been conducted in far too tame a manner" and was "the most respectable strike
ever known in the history of Belfast."[22] Geehan's description of the
strike as "respectable" might seem odd, given the violence surrounding the dispute. It was the tactics of the union leadership, however,
that he had in mind when he made the comment—namely their
failure to call out other groups of workers in solidarity with the railwaymen. Here Geehan was like a general without an army: neither
he nor the RWGs were in a position to make a decisive impact on
the outcome of the strike.

Neither the intervention of the IRA nor the Communists was
strong enough to tip the balance in favor of the workers. A more serious concern for GNR bosses came when dockers in Belfast began
to refuse to handle any "diverted goods" that would have otherwise
been destined for GNR trains.[23] The *Belfast Telegraph* reported that
the "refusal of the Dockers at Belfast to handle linen goods con-
signed from the country to cross-Channel ports for transhipment
overseas is seriously affecting manufacturers and merchants in pro-
vincial centers and it is probable that several thousand workers will
be thrown idle next week if there is not a change in the situation."[24]
This caused a number of heated scenes, with the RUC demanding
the diverted goods "at the point of the revolver."[25] By the end of February, however, over one hundred thousand tons of goods were held
up at the docks.[26] The dockers were resolute in their solidarity with
the railwaymen. When a number of GNR lorries carrying diverted
grain attempted to leave Belfast docks, 160 workers immediately
ceased work. Following attempts by management to use themselves
as scab labor, the dockers responded with stones and paving stones,
smashing windows and injuring a number of the scab lorry men.
One of the drivers collapsed and had to be taken to the Royal Vic-
toria Hospital.[27] A resolution was passed at a meeting of the Amalgamated Transport Workers' Union calling on the union's National
Executive to call out ten thousand dockers and carters in sympathy
with the railway workers.[28] If enacted, it could have brought the

economy in Northern Ireland to a standstill. In the end, the trade union leaders in London decided against initiating solidarity action, and the dockers were never called out on strike.[29]

The failure of the unions to back calls for solidarity action left the railwaymen isolated. By March, some two months into the strike, both the union leadership and the railway companies had grown weary, and negotiations began on a possible deal. The feeling among the strikers themselves was still militant, and on March 24 thousands of people marched in Belfast in solidarity with the rail workers. Eventually, the union leadership accepted a deal that would see the men take a cut in wages of 7 percent. It was a partial defeat for the railwaymen, and some workers stayed out on unofficial action in protest. Nevertheless, the final wage cut was only half of what the rail companies originally wanted, and the railwaymen had stopped a more general assault on working conditions.

The importance of the strike was in its political implications. The strike had once more brought a mainly Protestant workforce into confrontation with the Orange State and had sought and won solidarity from Southern workers in the process. The strike had posed a challenge, albeit in a limited sense, to both the Northern and Southern states, and it had brought workers from across Ireland together in a single struggle. The fact that a majority Protestant workforce did not react unfavorably to the direct intervention of the IRA was testament to the fluidity of politics at the time.

The railway strike was a sign that the vibrant militancy on display during the relief riots was not confined to a single issue. One result was that a number of the workers joined the RWGs, further widening the Communists' base in the working class. On June 3 and 4, 1933, the Dublin Total Abstinence Society met in Leinster Street, Dublin. Unbeknownst to the religiously inclined owners of the building, this gathering of supposed teetotallers was in fact the inaugural conference of the Communist Party of Ireland (CPI), hosted under a fake name for fear of reprisals by right-wing Catholics. The Communists hoped that this would be the springboard for the development of a mass revolutionary organization in Ireland. Seán Murray was elected its general secretary and Jim Larkin Jr. its chairman, while Belfast members Tommy Geehan and Betty Sinclair were both elected to its central committee.

All was not well, however. The combined forces of the Protestant and Catholic churches as well as the Unionist and Irish states were working against any chance the Communists had of growing. In reality, the CPI was formed in an atmosphere of increasing repression. On March 29, 1933, the CPI headquarters in Dublin was invaded by hundreds of anticommunist Catholics, who set the building alight. In Belfast, the Unionist state was increasing its efforts to isolate the Communists and their unemployed campaign. A march organized on the first anniversary of the ODR riots from Dublin to Belfast was blocked, and on October 17, 1933, the RUC raided and wrecked the party's offices, arresting and jailing three prominent CPI leaders.[30] In addition, police raided a number of members' homes. On the same day they ransacked the party offices, police in Belfast forced their way into the home of Communist John Montgomery—a former British Army soldier who had served three years in France during the Great War—in Trillick Street in the east of the city, where Montgomery's son, an active member of the YCL, had erected a small hut to store Communist literature and organize meetings. Montgomery insisted that their literature "was not banned, as they were advocating the cause of the down-trodden." At least one person was pleased to see the RUC, however: John Montgomery's wife told the police that it was "near time you came, they have my heart broken talking communism all night." When her son awoke, Mrs. Montgomery reportedly "went into the room and commenced to beat the son" before the "young Montgomery ran down stairs and out of the house."[31] There was no doubt that being involved in the CPI in Belfast was a perilous undertaking. One republican and socialist writer later claimed that during this period "many [CPI members] were to lose their employment after the 'friendly call' from the political police to the boss."[32]

There were also tensions within the Belfast branch of the CPI. Geehan's popularity among the unemployed was indisputable. But it would appear that he was less successful at following the tight discipline of the CPI, a tendency that would often cause tension with the Dublin-based leadership and their allies in Belfast, who were working to remove him from positions of influence. The tensions were evident in this 1933 internal report sent to Moscow:

> The local organisation is hampered by factional divisions also. Comrade Geehan ignores the party and has hindered collective work, especially in regard to the unemployed movement. The central committee meeting after the [Congress] decided that Geehan be removed from the leadership of the unemployed movement and brought into other work. Johnstone's report suggests that [Geehan] is not carrying out the party decision and will possibly leave the party.[33]

Geehan refused to quit his position in the unemployed movement or the CPI. Neither his skillful leadership nor his stature among Belfast's working class was sufficient, however, to prevent the escalating repression of the movement. In 1934, the unemployed campaign supported by the Communists (now known as the Irish Unemployed Movement) organized another rally to mark the second anniversary of the ODR riots. The RUC, confident that the movement was now weakened, were content to advise Stormont that banning the march would be futile: "[The RUC] seems to anticipate that the demonstration this year will be of little importance and, in the absence of full information as to its size, [is] rather doubtful that it should be prohibited."[34] The government, however, was in no mood to take any chances, and an order was issued prohibiting the demonstration. In the end, perhaps as few as 150 people attended. In Gresham Street in Belfast's city center, Tommy Geehan took to a chair to announce that he would read out a "resolution in defiance of the police."[35] The police intervened to stop Geehan, whereupon he called out for "three cheers for the unemployed." Geehan was charged and convicted for the incident. A later appeal was quashed.[36]

The fracturing of the unemployed movement and the ebb in class struggle following the defeat of the railway strike now opened the door for other forces on the right to seize the initiative. Despite the optimism of the Communists, sectarianism had not disappeared but had instead only retreated temporarily. Sectarian ideas and organizations still existed in working-class areas, and the potential existed for these groups to be harnessed to counter the rise of the Left. Chief among those trying to reinvigorate sectarian tensions were Unionist politicians. Just days after the ODR riots, Prime Minister Craig attempted to win back a section of Protestant supporters by ensuring them that "Ours is a Protestant Government and I am an Orangeman." He continued with this theme in the following weeks:

> I have always said I am an Orangeman first and a politician and member of Parliament afterwards. . . . All I boast is that we are a Protestant Parliament and a Protestant State. Therefore, it is undoubtedly our duty and our privilege, and always will be, to see that those appointed by us possess the most unimpeachable loyalty to the King and Constitution. This is my whole object in carrying on a Protestant government for a Protestant people.[37]

Craig was not alone in using sectarianism to break working-class unity. Basil Brooke, the Unionist MP and later Northern Ireland prime minister, told a gathering of Orangemen that he would not have a Catholic about the place, while another Unionist MP, J. A. McCormick, went further by arguing that the Catholic population should be prevented from increasing:

> Thousands of Roman Catholics had been added to the population either by birth rate or the adoption of this province as their home. In many places Protestant majorities were now minorities and at that rate of increase twenty years would see the Church of Rome in power. Instead of waiting and telling them to get out means should be taken to prevent them from coming in.[38]

This heightening of sectarian tensions was not opposed in any organizational form by the Left, which put all its faith in the resurgence of a working-class movement based on bread-and-butter issues to the exclusion of organizing an ideological opposition to sectarianism. In neglecting to confront the gathering sectarian offensive directly they left unchallenged the notion that Catholics were to blame for unemployment, paving the way for the rearticulation of class grievances through the reactionary narrative of sectarianism. It was a crucial mistake, and one that meant that the Unionist government was able to claw back many of the key concessions that they had been compelled to agree to in October 1932. For example, the new relief rates granted after the ODR strike were paid to some workers and not to others, and in the following year the government dramatically scaled back its overall expenditure on relief.

Anger over unemployment was once again on the rise from 1934 to 1935. In the absence of any real action by a united unemployed movement, however, attempts were made by forces on the right to channel anger against the government in a sectarian direction. Hard-line Unionists began to demand the intensification of discrimination against Catholics in order to alleviate the plight of Protestants. Sir Joseph Davison, the Grand Master of the Orange Order, summed up this new line of argument. "When will the Protestant employers of Northern Ireland recognise their duty to their Protestant brothers and sisters and employ them to the exclusion of Roman Catholics?" he asked. "It is time Protestant employers realised that whenever a Roman Catholic is brought into their employment it means one Protestant vote less. I suggest the slogan should be 'Protestants employ Protestants.'"[39]

The slogan of "Protestants employ Protestants" and, as historian Graham Walker puts it, "the relatively widespread belief in the Protestant community that Catholics were taking over important jobs" combined to create the environment for a renewal of sectarian tensions.[40] This did not automatically translate into renewed support for the Unionist Party—instead the chief beneficiaries were sectarian forces on the ground, epitomized by the rise of the Ulster Protestant League (UPL), an organization set up in 1931 to "safeguard the employment of Protestants." The UPL opposed any unity between Catholics and Protestants and in 1931 had attacked an unemployment march organized by the RWGs. It opposed the ODR strike of 1932 in equal measure:

> We deplore that these unfortunate conditions were used as a
> cloak by the Communist Sinn Féin element to attempt to start a
> revolution in our province. We also greatly deplore that some of

our loyal Protestant unemployed were misled to such an extent that they associated themselves with enemies of their faith and principles. We congratulate the Government of Northern Ireland on the firm steps that they have taken to preserve law and order in our city.[41]

Branches of the UPL began to appear in Belfast after the ODR strike. Its main appeal as an organization was that it demanded jobs for Protestants and an end to government "pandering" to the Catholic minority. The UPL argued that Catholics had infiltrated the state and that key positions were given to them within the police force and the civil service. Its paper, the *Ulster Protestant*, carried numerous articles relating to preferential treatment given to Catholics in the labor market and related stories of Protestants ostensibly being sacked from jobs for being "loyal," in contrast to the treatment of Catholics, who were kept on despite displays of "disloyalty."[42] Ironically, the discontent that fueled the ODR riots was the same discontent that had fueled the rise of the UPL—the difference being that the ODR strike had firmly pointed the finger of blame at those at the top (the Unionist government), while the UPL pointed the finger at those across the divide (the Catholic community).

The UPL was led by sections of the Protestant middle class, including the Presbyterian ministers Reverend Samuel Hanna and Reverend H. H. Aitcheson, and by right-wing representatives from the better-off sections of the labor movement, such as Joseph McConnell, who worked as a foreman. The *Ulster Protestant* carried the slogan "Vote Protestant, Buy Protestant, Sell Protestant, Be Protestant," which gave the UPL some appeal to the squeezed Protestant middle class. Its main base of support, however, was among the Protestant unemployed, who felt aggrieved by their treatment at the hands of the Orange State. If anything, this appeal offered unemployed Protestants the promise of entitlement to privilege, rather than an actually existing privilege. As the historian A. C. Hepburn argues:

> The UPL . . . represented a loose alliance of these evangelicals with the poorest elements of the Protestant community, most of whom were outside the trade union movement . . . designed to appeal

to Protestants who were in conflict with the police over law and order questions, or who were in direct competition with Catholics for employment, or were unemployed, rather than to skilled workers in industries from which Catholics were virtually excluded.[43]

The UPL had the support of important sections of the Unionist establishment. Basil Brooke spoke at many of its meetings and the UPL was frequently given free access to the Unionist Party headquarters for its events. However, they were not simply a creation of the state. Despite their links to the government, the UPL was an independent force representing a distortion of class discontent with the government through the reactionary politics of loyalism. The UPL was in its own way an anti-government force: its trajectory was to push the government to the right by demanding an intensified program of discrimination against Catholics to the benefit of Protestants. As Munck and Rolston argue, "The UPL represented the extreme of popular sectarianism . . . a relatively independent force, sometimes meshing well with government wishes, sometimes clashing with them, and sometimes a harbinger of the government's own subsequent sectarian actions."[44]

The weeks and months after the ODR riots witnessed notable growth in numbers and influence for the UPL in working-class Protestant areas. However, this did not mean that working-class unity was dead or that the opportunities for the Communists had disappeared. It did, however, mean that the newly formed CPI would have to fight with the UPL for support within the Protestant working class. The UPL worked hard to stem the growth of the CPI and would often disrupt its meetings. A favored tactic was to beat a Lambeg drum (a large drum used primarily by Unionists, particularly in Orange Order parades) during Communist street meetings to make the speeches inaudible. Depending on the balance of forces, the UPL would sometimes physically attack CPI members, particularly those out selling the party's paper. A protracted battle—both physical and ideological—ensued between the forces of communism and loyalism within Protestant working-class areas throughout the 1930s. Despite loyalist opposition, the CPI succeeded in forming branches in Protestant working-class heartlands such as the Shankill and Newtownards Roads. Many of these Protestant recruits—including Betty Sinclair, Billy McCullough, and Davey Scarborough—would form the bulk of the leadership of the Communists for the next few decades.

The Communists were not the only radical force in Belfast. The ODR struggle had a major impact on another organization, the IRA, as exemplified by their involvement in the railway dispute. The riots in 1932 had caught the leadership of the IRA unawares, causing consternation and soul-searching among some of its membership. Recruitment to the IRA was slow during the ODR campaign, with one of its Belfast officers commenting that "one would have thought the recent trouble in the city would have brought large numbers into the army."[45] A schism had opened up within its membership over the relationship between the national question and social issues. The main base of the IRA in Belfast was among the nationalist poor and unemployed, and the political perceptions of many of its members underwent a process of radicalization after the ODR strike. Joe Cahill, later a leading figure in the IRA, described how the strike made him "think about the causes of division, why they existed. I had a lot of social ideas in my head at that time."[46] IRA volunteer Jack Brady recalls that at the time "it was debated with hindsight, when the Outdoor Relief strike had petered out, did we miss the boat or did we not, should we have got involved in it or not, gone on the streets and opened up."[47] In the end the consensus was that "they would not pass up such an opportunity again."[48]

The IRA involvement in the railway strike was both an effort to regain lost ground and an attempt to appease its leftward-shifting rank and file. However, the tensions between the more conservative IRA leadership and the left-wing members within its ranks continued to grow, leading to a split in March 1934 with several of its best-known members, including Army Council member Peadar O'Donnell, leaving and setting up a new organization—the Republican Congress. The Congress grew quickly from its inception and won the support of thousands of people, both North and South. It was backed by a number of key members of the IRA and the republican women's organization, the Cumann na mBan, as well as labor and trade union figures and some well-known radicals like Roddy and Nora Connolly (James Connolly's son and daughter). The Congress also won the support of a section of the Protestant working class. O'Donnell helped set up James Connolly Workers Republican Clubs in Protestant districts like the Shankill Road, and the Congress won the support of the Northern Ireland Socialist Party, a mainly Protestant organization affiliated with the NILP that had grown out of the ODR struggle and helped further the presence of the organization in the Protestant working-class districts of Belfast. In May 1934, the Congress called a protest at the Custom House steps in Belfast over unemployment. This attracted three thousand people, the largest gathering of the unemployed since October 1932.

Not everyone agreed on what type of organization the Republican Congress should attempt to build, and there was debate within the group about what exactly they were fighting for. A division emerged between those who saw the Congress as a means to reinvigorate republicanism and those who saw it as means to develop a new, more radical and explicitly socialist organization. While republicans such as Peadar O'Donnell were serious in their commitment to social issues, they still held on to the project of building the republican movement as an all-class alliance. O'Donnell and his supporters argued that the Republican Congress should be an alliance between representatives of the IRA, the rank and file of Fianna Fáil (the main nationalist party in the Free State), labor, trade unions, and small farmers' groups. The Congress should be an all-Ireland body, they argued, which would unite all those who supported the fight for "the Republic." Other IRA members, such as Mick Price, the IRA's director of training, argued that this did not go far enough and called instead for the Congress to build a revolutionary movement fighting for a socialist Workers' Republic. As the Republican Congress began to develop, this contradiction remained unsolved.[49]

The CPI joined the Republican Congress. The Communists had considerable influence over rank-and-file republicans. Indeed, a report on a national meeting of the RWGs in November 1932 noted that the "majority of [members] are members also of the IRA."[50] A later internal document filed in 1933 suggested that the CPI's "rural locals are composed almost 100 percent of IRA men."[51] The intervention of the CPI into this debate could have been crucial in winning the movement to a socialist position that would hold out some appeal to both Protestant and Catholic workers. Certainly, had the Congress been launched in 1932, this is precisely what the Communists would have argued. However, while the CPI threw itself into building the Republican Congress, the theoretical perspective that informed its activity was undergoing a drastic change. The rise of Hitler and the crushing of the Communist Party of Germany had laid waste to the "class against class" policy, which had denied the possibility of any joint action between Communists and German Social Democrats to resist the rise of Nazism. Simultaneously, Stalin was working to tighten his grip over the international Communist movement, and his allies were arguing for a shift in policy toward what came to be termed the "Popular Front" strategy, an alliance between Communists and progressive supporters of capitalism, such as reformists and liberals. British socialist Duncan Hallas outlines the depth of this shift: "For Stalin to consolidate his power internationally . . . the Comintern was now to be swung, by Stalin's agents, to a position well to the right of the social democratic parties, to a position of class collaboration."[52]

This shift in policy would have consequences for the tactical approach adopted by the CPI in relation to the Republican Congress. The CPI perspective was no longer to unite workers North and South in the struggle for a Workers' Republic but rather to fight initially for a capitalist republic, after which the struggle for socialism could begin. Seán Murray, the party's general secretary, summed up the CPI position during the debate: "Congress should stand for an Irish Republic. I say you cannot smash capitalism until you get rid of British imperialism."[53] At a meeting of the Congress in Rathmines in September 1934, a debate raged between the O'Donnell and George Gilmore faction—which called for a broad republican movement—and the faction led by Michael Price—arguing instead for an openly socialist party fighting for a Workers' Republic. Price and his supporters argued that the slogan of a "Workers' Republic" clearly distinguished them from both Éamon De Valera's Fianna Fáil and the IRA. They also argued that the slogan included Protestant workers in the North and explained to them the difference between the socialist idea of a republic and the conservative, Catholic state that held power in the South at that time. Nora Connolly argued that "it is the phrase 'Irish Republic' that separated us from the mass of workers in the north," while other speakers suggested that they could win Protestants to a Workers' Republic but could not win them to a capitalist Irish Republic. The CPI sided with O'Donnell and Gilmore and swayed the vote over the issue in their favor: 99 votes to 84 in favor of the Irish Republic resolution. Nora Connolly blamed the Stalinist politics of CPI for the decision: "The Communists did not want the Republican Congress. They were out for a United Front, but this was something Russia wanted, not what we wanted."[54] Patrick Byrne, at one time the joint secretary of the Republican Congress, recalled that he was in favor of the Workers' Republic resolution but voted against it out of loyalty to Gilmore and O'Donnell. After the vote was recorded, Price turned to Byrne and said "You have put the revolution back 100 years." "Looking back," wrote Byrne, "I think it was a great mistake that we did not go for a Workers' Party."[55]

By proposing to move forward on the basis of a narrow nationalist program, the Republican Congress effectively jettisoned its Protestant support base. "From then on," according to Byrne, "the movement lost momentum. Trade Union support melted away, the Connollys and others retreated into the oblivion of the Labour Party. Roddy Connolly was distressed, as indeed most of us were. Nora took it very hard."[56] This would have disastrous results for the CPI as well. The party had developed a base in both Protestant and Catholic areas as an organization that rejected both the Unionist state in the North and the clerical Catholic state in the South. Both of these positions were of equal importance and positioned the party to appeal to both Catholic and Protestant workers. Because of the relative backwardness of the Irish state in the South, both economically and culturally, it was unlikely that Protestant workers were ever going to fight to become a part of it. By calling for a Workers' Republic, the Communists could appeal to Protestant workers and alleviate concerns that they were simply looking for an extension of the rotten state in the South, where the Catholic Church was the dominant force in society. On June 18, 1934, at the Wolfe Tone commemoration in Bodenstown, organized annually to remember Wolfe Tone, the founder of modern Irish republicanism, around five hundred Belfast members of the Republican Congress "composed largely of Protestants and Presbyterians drawn in the main from the . . . Orange districts of Belfast" marched behind a banner that read "Shankill Road Belfast Branch. Break the Connection with Capitalism. Connolly's Message Our Ideal. On to the Workers' Republic." Unfortunately, the presence of the contingent, and the anti-capitalist and communist content of their banner, alarmed more conservative nationalist elements of the IRA, who rushed to remove the banner. Fierce fighting followed between the marchers from Belfast and the IRA members, leaving a bitter taste in the mouths of many of the Protestant marchers. The incident was testament to the fact that Protestants could certainly be won to a socialist anti-partitionist position, but that ultimately this was not possible within the confines of a nationalist project.

Their retreat from the principle of a Workers' Republic would signal the decline of the CPI within the Protestant working class. Unfortunately, this was also the very moment that forces to the right were beginning to surge. Throughout 1934 and 1935 the UPL had continued to grow, becoming more violent and confrontational as their ranks swelled. In 1934, they organized large protests against the decision by the authorities to allow the Catholic Truth Society festival to be held in Belfast. The UPL painted this as an example of government softness toward Catholics, and they held meetings and protests throughout the city. After one such meeting on May 24, 1934, large mobs attacked Nationalist areas, causing considerable damage. Throughout the year of 1935, the UPL escalated their campaign against the Catholic population. On May 10, 1935, the government was forced to impose a curfew after large mobs attacked Catholic districts and tried to oust Catholic workers from mixed workplaces following celebrations in Protestant areas marking

George V's Silver Jubilee. In the following weeks the UPL became increasingly active, organizing large meetings and parades, often close to Catholic areas of Belfast in order to maximize tensions.[57]

As the annual Twelfth of July parade in 1935 approached, concern grew that a full-scale sectarian riot might develop. The Unionist government had created a monster that it could no longer control, and was growing worried about the consequences of the instability on the streets. In an effort to regain some semblance of control, Richard Dawson Bates issued a proclamation on June 17 banning all processions in the city. The Grand Master of the Orange Order replied to this by issuing a statement which declared that "no government would prevent Orangemen from marching," and on June 23, the Orange Order organized an illegal parade through the city to defy the ban. The Order had called Bates's bluff, and in a classic case of the tail wagging the dog, the minister was forced to lift the ban on parades.

On July 12, around forty thousand Orangemen marched through the streets of Belfast. There was some violence as the parade passed the Catholic Markets area but it was not until the evening, when Orangemen marched home, that the real trouble broke out. As the North Belfast lodges passed a small Catholic enclave housing around seventeen hundred people, rioting broke out. Reports have differed as to who actually started the trouble, but as Hepburn argues, "The immediate order of events is insignificant. Whether the Orangemen were ambushed [or] they invaded the streets is disputed. . . . Whatever the balance of blame for the events on the 12th, it is clear that the Catholics were more often on the receiving end in the days that followed."[58]

The rioting in North Belfast was the signal for a full-scale pogrom against the Catholic community across Belfast. The following day Protestant mobs invaded vulnerable Catholic areas and forced families from their homes. Loyalists also targeted religiously mixed areas such as the Old Lodge, near the Shankill, which was virtually cleansed of Catholic families between July 15 and 18. The state had completely lost control, and loyalist mobs rampaged through the city for the next ten days. By the end of the trouble, 2,241 Catholics had been evicted from their homes, along with a few hundred Protestants, some of whom were the victims of personal vendettas or reprisals for living in mixed marriages. It was clear where the blame for the violence lay. According to James Kelly, "City Coroner, T. E. Alexander, commenting on the deaths of the victims put the blame fairly and squarely on the unchristian utterance of the government politicians in the two years' campaign to divide and rule."[59]

This was not the end of the violence, however. As the factory holiday period came to an end and people returned to work, hundreds of Catholics were intimidated away from their workplaces. Unlike the pogroms of the past, the instigators of this intimidation were not Protestant workers based in particular workplaces but gangs of unemployed on the outside, who gathered at the gates of the shipyards to prevent Catholics from getting to work.

The effect of the riots had a paralyzing effect on the Left, including the Communist Party, which had called on the Trades Council to call a general strike, but to no effect. The CPI claimed that they would launch a Workers' Defence Force to counter "Craigavon's storm troopers," but nothing came of it. However, not all of their members stood by passively. Tommy Geehan, who was himself expelled from his home by loyalists in the midst of the rioting, emerged from the rubble to lead the resistance. At Glenard, adjacent to the small Catholic mill district of Ardoyne, a housing estate designed to be "a 100 per cent Protestant colony" was nearing the end of construction.[60] Geehan organized around 150 families who had been forced out of their homes to go into the estate and occupy the houses. The Catholic hierarchy, expressing fears that "Glenard is being captured by Bolshevism," bought forty-eight of the houses to be distributed to people it deemed to be of suitable character.[61] Geehan was later sentenced to fourteen days' imprisonment for inciting a crowd to resist eviction. He was the only political figure to come before the courts as a result of the vicious and prolonged sectarian rioting, no doubt a belated punishment for his role in the events of 1932.[62]

The 1935 riots were not simply an explosion of irrational hatred against Catholics, though this certainly played its part. The riots were the culmination of three years of sectarian agitation on the part of the Unionists, who used anger in Protestant areas over economic degradation as a fuel to stoke the sectarian fire. The inability of the Left to sustain an effective class-based movement capable of winning better conditions for working people, combined with their refusal to organize a sustained challenge to the sectarian narrative that "Catholics are to blame," created a situation in which growing forces on the right worked to exploit deep anger over economic issues and drive it in a sectarian direction. As Mike Milotte has put it, a "defeated working class was more easily turned against itself than a victorious one could possibly have been."[63]

Newspaper reports from 1935 suggest that beneath the anti-Catholic hysteria of the time, the riots were created by the economic desperation of working-class Protestants over jobs and housing, justified by the sectarian notion that Protestants should be provided for before Catholics. There was a sense among the rioters that by evicting a Catholic family from a house, a Protestant family could move in: "We are taking a house for my sister," one boy responded when asked what he was doing. This was true too of the expulsions of Catholics from work—it was unemployed Protestants in the main who expelled them, inspired by the notion that they were reclaiming jobs that were rightfully theirs.[64]

It would be wrong, then, to see the 1932 riots and the 1935 riots as something completely different—one the expression of class discontent with the government, the other an expression of cultural animosity between two communities. The truth is that the fundamental conditions underlying the deep anger fueling the riots were the same in 1935 as they had been in 1932—poverty, unemployment, and a belief that the government was not providing for people. The difference between the two riots was the way in which the anger over these issues was expressed. Ultimately, the crucial element that determined the manifest form of this anger—either as vicious sectarianism or as unity against the Unionist elite—was the intervention of organized political forces.

The North's fledgling Communist movement barely managed to survive this turn in events. Debased, confused, and scattered, the Communists became a shadow of their former selves. Together the failures of the CPI in this period and the effects of the violence were to have a devastating impact on the group. After the riots, only twenty members showed up for a Belfast aggregate meeting to discuss the future of the party. In 1932, the RWGs, with all their faults, had effectively combined an appeal for class unity with a concrete movement on the streets that could deliver change. In 1935, the CPI had abandoned this position in favor of Irish nationalism and the liberal politics of the all-class alliance, leaving the field wide open for forces like the UPL to take the initiative. The effect of the Stalinist turn toward the Popular Front left the party completely disoriented, wrecking any chance of capitalizing on the uniquely favorable position that the 1932 riots had offered them. The opportunity on offer, "if not for making the socialist revolution," was, according to Milotte, "at least for gaining a foothold in important sections of the working class."[65]

The ODR strike, in this new context, became an increasingly hazy and receding landmark in an otherwise barren political landscape. Some left-wing activists searched for new pastures: the Spanish Civil War became a beacon for many, with scores travelling to serve in the anti-fascist International Brigades. If it was the experience of the ODR strike that inspired many people to join the Left, it was the bitter taste of defeat that motivated many to look elsewhere for the hope of political transformation. They travelled to fight Franco and his fascists, to fight for freedom and democracy. Above all else, perhaps, they fought to keep alive the flame of hope that appeared to be all but extinguished at home. Their journey was, in equal parts, an act of incredible heroism and of profound desperation.

At home, those who remained to fly the red flag faced their own difficulties. The dramatic rise in sectarianism was bad enough, but this was greatly exacerbated by the continuing effects of Stalinist distortion within the movement, as is evidenced in the twists and turns imposed on the party by Moscow throughout the remainder of the decade. In 1932 the CPI had followed the "Third Period" line from the Comintern. This strategy had its faults—including a tendency toward ultra-left posturing and a sectarian attitude toward supporters of laborism—but it did allow the party to develop the kind of militant mass movement that was needed during the ODR strike. By 1934, however, the CPI had executed a dramatic about-turn, implementing the new Popular Front strategy that led the party to capitulate to Irish nationalism during the Republican Congress debate, abandoning much of its potential Protestant base in the process.

During the Second World War the CPI's membership began to recover, but on a very different political basis from what it was in the 1930s, and in reaction to yet another ideological about-turn. Following the entry of the Soviet Union into the war, the party became the most enthusiastic supporters of the British war effort (despite having been vocal opponents of the war during Stalin's brief détente with Nazi Germany). In the process, they effectively dropped any criticism of the Unionist state and abandoned the notion of independent class politics that had informed their success in the ODR strike. The party began to grow—particularly in Protestant areas—owing to its adoption of pro-British jingoism, but the effects of its political degeneration were significant. When large-scale industrial unrest broke out during wartime, uniting thousands of rank-and-file Protestant and Catholic workers in the process, the CPI opposed it, insisting that the strikes were unpatriotic and should be called off. During the war they renamed themselves the Communist Party of Northern Ireland, an important distinction that indicated the party's willingness to accommodate itself to the partitionist sentiment within the Protestant working class, rather than challenge it as party members had previously.

The extent to which the failures of the Irish Communists can be blamed on the nefarious influence of Moscow is a point of debate among historians. Some have argued that Moscow's role was negligible: the Irish Communists largely paid lip service to them, it is argued, and at times even privately expressed disquiet with Comintern dictates.[66] Others suggest that Moscow's intervention was largely positive—indeed that the RWGs were unlikely to "have survived for very long without the Comintern."[67] It is true that the usually right-wing inspired caricature of the Communists as glad-handed puppets of their Russian paymasters is usually far off the mark. And it is certainly the case that the Irish Communists were capable of self-initiative, of responding to events on the ground as they shifted—as their impressive role in the ODR strike will attest. This initiative, however, was always geared toward an overall political perspective that was set elsewhere. The relationship was, to appropriate a phrase from the historian of fascism Ian Kershaw, one of "working towards Moscow," wherein the activity of the Communists was ultimately configured to fit with the foreign policy interests of the USSR, regardless of the impact on the movement in Ireland. The bewildering zigzags that that this produced—from ultra-left posturing to popular-frontism in a matter of years, then from ultra-left posturing to soft unionism thereafter—and the disorientating effect that this produced in the ranks of the Left, had a severely debilitating impact on the development of the revolutionary movement in Ireland. The Communists were, therefore, like a woodsman travelling home in the dark: they followed their instincts and experience, certainly, but always angled against the constellations in the sky that they hoped would point them in the right direction. Undoubtedly, the brightest star for the Communists was Moscow, and such an orientation led to misdirection and disaster, time and time again.

The decline of the Communist movement—both qualitatively and quantitatively—is perhaps best typified by the fortunes of its most capable leader, Tommy Geehan, who resigned from the CPI in 1938, during a period when the party dropped its opposition to partition and grew closer to unionism. The journalist James Kelly, who had covered Geehan's exploits during the ODR strike, saw him in 1942 in workman overalls, inauspiciously drinking a pint with some shipyard workers in the Monico bar on Rosemary Street. "From the lofty heights of a man of the moment," wrote Kelly, with unconcealed despondency, "he slipped back into the ranks of the ordinary individual in the street, a forgotten man."[68] Tragically, the hope of a better future for the working class had slipped away too.

CONCLUSION

T en years before the ODR riots, on May 22, 1922, loyalist hard-liner and Unionist MP for Belfast West William Twaddell was walking on Garfield Street in the city center near to the outfitter's shop he owned a short distance away. It was here that Twaddell was confronted by a number of gunmen who fired between six and eight shots, killing him at the scene. The death of Twaddell sent shockwaves throughout the establishment, and the response of the state was swift and brutal: the newly established Special Powers Act was for the first time put into full effect, with hundreds of people interned without trial, many of them on board the *Argenta*, a purpose-built prison ship moored off the coast of Carrickfergus.

The identity of Twaddell's assailants was never fully confirmed. Many arrests were made, but no one was ultimately convicted. The attack had been carried out by members of the IRA's Carrick Hill Company, though it was unclear who, if anyone, had sanctioned it. In an effort to get to the bottom of the matter, the IRA held its own internal investigation. Sean Montgomery, a member of the organization at the time, recalls being questioned at the time over the killing:

> I was ordered to report to Division Headquarters and I was ac-cused of the shooting. I told the staff I had nothing to do with it and I was threatened by Seamus Woods and another officer. When I could not answer Sean Keenan and J. McKeever started soft-soaping, I was about two hours telling them I had nothing to do with it but I thought I had an idea who had done the job.[1]

Montgomery was insistent that he had not carried out the attack. He did have an idea, however, of who might be to blame: "With the Vice OC Brigade I went to a Billiard Hall where the two men were.

I told them I was going through a tough time so they said I was right, it was them. Both are dead now. T. Geehan and P. McAleese."[2] Could it be that the "T. Geehan" referred to here by Sean Montgomery is the same Tommy Geehan of the Revolutionary Workers Groups? One historian of Belfast republicanism during this period, Jimmy McDermott, suggests that there is other circumstantial evidence that points to that conclusion:

> Sean Montgomery's account opens up the intriguing possibility of Tommy Geehan, the leader of the future Revolutionary Marxist Groups [sic] and prime mover in the Outdoor Relief Movement of the 1930s as a suspect in the Twaddell murder case. Certainly Geehan, at 22, was the right age and he did live in 27 Hanover Street, close to Carrick Hill, but it is unclear whether he was a republican at that time.[3]

McDermott does not close the door on the possibility of Geehan's involvement, only holding back for lack of clear evidence that Geehan had ever been a republican. We can now fill in this important missing piece. Geehan's Cadre File, long stored in Moscow but now accessible outside of Russia, indicates otherwise.[4] He was asked in a 1930 questionnaire whether he had ever been a member of another political organization; his reply was that he had been a member of the republican movement from 1919 to 1923—before leaving because he "disagreed with the policy of [the] formation of the Free State"—which would place him in the organization at the time of Twaddell's killing. Indeed, Geehan himself was never an avowed pacifist. He had been investigated by the RUC for making a "seditious" speech at a meeting of the West Belfast Labour Party on Peel Street in 1927, when he told his audience that he would be prepared to kill for the cause, an assertion noted by the RUC officer assigned to transcribe the meeting: "[Geehan] said he was opposed to a war which was not for the purpose of protecting the interests of workers. He was not opposed to killing if it were necessary in the interests of the workers, nor would he hesitate to take up a gun in the defence of his class, and it might be necessary in future."[5]

Montgomery's suspicions about the individuals involved in Twaddell's death—reinforced by the circumstantial evidence and clarified by the evidence of Geehan's membership in the IRA—means that we can say with some confidence that the future Communist was in all likelihood involved in the assassination of the prominent Unionist MP. If true, there has scarcer been a more astounding twist of fate in the storied history of Belfast: Tommy Geehan, the widely respected leader of the most significant period of Protestant and Catholic working-class unity in the city's history, was once an IRA gunman, implicated in one of Belfast's most sensational political murders. Superficially, at least, the story would seem to undermine Geehan's credibility as the leading figure in a movement that drew workers together from across the sectarian divide. In truth, it dramatically underlines the single most important lesson of 1932: that our past does not have to be our future, and that people and politics can and do change.

Was the kind of political and personal transformation which Geehan underwent between the early 1920s and the mid-1930s unique? A parallel story—one that concluded more than twelve hundred miles from Belfast—would suggest that it was not. On March 14, 1937, a small detachment of anti-Franco republican forces found themselves hemmed in on the Valencia Road in Spain, outnumbered and outgunned. "Wave after wave of Fascist troops hurled themselves on our lines," one participant recalled, "especially on our left flank, in an attempt to break through."[6] By noon their lines had been broken, the Fascists were advancing, and the battle looked to be lost. As it happened, republican machine guns had been poorly positioned and were having little effect on the enemy. The possibility of being decimated by fascist forces loomed, and the commandant of the republican forces that day, Liam Tumilson, took immediate measures to attempt to reverse the situation. Rushing to a small hill overlooking the battlefield to assess the republicans' predicament and issue instructions to the troops, the commandant was struck by a sniper's bullet, dying instantly.

Tumilson was a thirty-three-year-old Belfast native. The son of Protestant parents and a former Orangeman himself, Tumilson was originally given the name William, but chose the Irish variation after a political radicalization in his early adult life. He had been a participant in the 1932 ODR strike, helping to organize the ODRWC in predominantly Protestant districts. Despite his background and his former membership of the Orange Order, his closest comrades insisted after his death that a "fitting memorial to Liam" would be the creation "of a free, happy and prosperous Workers' Republic." It is emblematic of the remarkable fluidity of this period that one person who began life as an Orangeman would die fighting for the cause of republicanism, while another who began his political journey in the ranks of the IRA would rise to become the leading figure in Belfast's greatest episode of Protestant and Catholic working-class unity. The thread that weaves these two tapestries together is, of course, the Outdoor Relief struggle.

These transformations beg the question of the larger significance of the 1932 agitation. Was the ODR struggle simply a fleeting aberration, a brief dalliance before the restoration of the old communal order of things? Possibly, but perhaps not. The remarkable political trajectories evident in the lives of Geehan and Tumilson, and a close reading of the wider period suggest instead that the events constituted something more than an insignificant blip on the timeline of modern Irish history. Far from a fleeting aberration, this was a deeply significant historical moment that marked a remarkable, though not permanent, reconfiguration of politics in the Depression years, including a significant degree of working-class unity that remained residually present for some years afterward. In truth, the ODR struggle threw up a number of contingent possibilities that we may lose sight of in looking back from the present day. Belfast eventually fell back into familiar grooves of sectarian division and disunity, but this was not a preordained outcome.

A more pertinent and revealing question to answer is how and by what means the unity of 1932 was broken, and whose interests the disruption of this common purpose served. A narrow, identity-based analysis—informed by the ethno-national determinism dominant in both academic history writing and in the sectarian assumptions underpinning the institutions of the modern Northern Ireland state—

would suggest that people simply returned from whence they came: back into their respective political and religious ghettoes. Such an analysis could only rest on a willful evasion of the actual historical record, however, which confirms that the unity created during the ODR agitation was deeply entrenched and that it did not simply dissipate in the days and months following the riots. The impressive growth of left-wing forces in working-class communities, the experience of the GNR railway strike, and the small but significant involvement of Protestants in the Republican Congress all attest to the power and resilience of the new anti-sectarian militancy. Any easy dismissal of the unity forged during the ODR agitation would also have to ignore the ways in which this unity came under determined assault through the pernicious, often violent intervention of powerful political forces—especially those grouped around the Unionist Party and the Orange Order and abetted by forces below them such as the Ulster Protestant League. The whole apparatus of the Orange State worked frantically to incite communal animosity and restore the status quo through a relentless campaign of sectarian agitation and scaremongering—culminating in the violent, hate-filled summer of 1935.

Enduring notions of identity and national allegiance, whether real or abstracted, cannot be allowed to whitewash the malevolent and divisive activities of those in power during the period. Given the space and time to develop on the basis of the solid start that mass protests had made possible, the unity achieved in 1932 could have deepened and expanded to chart a viable route of escape from Belfast's history of bitter division. That it did not was largely the result of a deliberate strategy of divide and rule—often directly imposed by the state—rather than any innate or pathological incapacity of the city's working class for overcoming deep-seated divisions. The relationship between the vitality of sectarian enmity and the stability of elite power was not lost either on Craigavon or on his government. On July 12, 1936, a year after the riots of 1935, he comforted his peers with the assurance that "Orangeism, Protestantism, and the Loyalist cause are more strongly entrenched than ever, and equally so is the government at Stormont."[7]

This emphasis on the remarkable achievements of the ODR agitation does not mean that the trajectory of events in the aftermath of the ODR riots is unimportant, however. Any serious analysis of the period will have to acknowledge that while the ODR campaign displayed the potential for working-class unity, it also revealed the power and persistence of communal division. Why was this the case? Some commentators—particularly those within the nationalist tradition, keen to write off the necessity of class politics—have suggested that the fundamental problem lay in the composition of the labor and unemployed movement itself. The Protestant working class, or at least key sections of it, proponents of this argument assert, were all too willing accomplices in the sectarian agitation led by big-house Unionist elites, and their alliance with Catholic workers in 1932 was of a pragmatic and temporary nature. Gerry Adams, the long-time president of Sinn Féin, has expressed this view himself:

> For the majority of people, that decade was a time of severe economic hardship. In Belfast, the Catholic and Protestant unemployed united briefly to demand work and social assistance. The "Outdoor Relief" strike was a sign of hope, but the unity achieved was soon broken. The unionist government, the Orange Order and the employers successfully used the tactic of divide and conquer. Protestant workers were reminded where their interests lay—with the state which would ensure that work, when it was available, would always go to them first.[8]

In essence, this argument flows from the notion that Protestants were a "privileged" caste within the working class, or an "aristocracy of labor" whose main community of interest was with Orange industrialists and politicians. It is an analysis, however, that does not withstand closer inspection. First, though it is true that Catholics continued to bear a disproportionate share of poverty and unemployment in the years after the ODR riots, it does not follow that this led to a significant improvement for their Protestant brothers and sisters. In truth, it is incontestable that the chief beneficiaries of the restoration of sectarianism were the economic elites in Northern

Ireland and in the Unionist government, for whom a risen and unified working class could only be viewed as a mortal threat.

Second, though Protestants did make up the majority of those in higher-paid skilled employment, this was not the main base of support for loyalist agitation in the years between 1932 and 1935. Indeed, as I argued in the preceeding chapter, the most fertile ground for the sectarian agitation of the UPL was not to be found within a privileged layer of skilled workers but instead within the ranks of the unemployed and among low-skilled Protestant laborers who had very little, if any, more than their Catholic counterparts. Loyalist agitation, therefore, grew in a period when unemployment was increasing after 1932 and reached its Depression-era peak. If it was material privilege that drove loyalism, it should have followed that its influence would have declined as unemployment rose, but this was plainly not the case. In truth, the ground on which class unity was built was the same ground on which the support for the UPL grew. The Communist agitation of 1932 was successful because it built a movement capable of convincing large numbers of working-class people that their lot was better served struggling together across the traditional divide. But this agitation was never combined with a political challenge to sectarian notions—including the vicious anti-Catholicism common within Orangeism—that continued to permeate throughout the class. For this reason, and because of the decline of the unemployment movement itself, loyalist forces were able to re-articulate class concerns and direct the frustrations of Protestant workers in a sectarian direction.

This was an eventuality that the Communists were wholly unprepared for. Even at their best, they presumed that a single period of working-class struggle would be enough to wipe out sectarianism. Though they never explicitly said it, they must have presumed too that such a movement would also wipe out or at least greatly diminish those organizations that espoused such politics. They saw no reason, therefore, to steel the unemployment movement, or even their own cadre, for a political fight with sectarianism. This was a crucial and costly mistake—one that left the movement toothless in the face of renewed loyalist agitation around unemployment, a problem that was only exacerbated as Communists themselves drifted further toward the politics of Irish nationalism during the era of the Republican Congress.

Why, then, did the struggles of 1932 not simply wash away all vestiges of sectarianism in an instant, as the RWGs had hoped? The answer is to be found within the complex relationship between practice, politics, and organization. Economic struggle, like that of the ODR dispute, can begin to break down barriers between previously divided workers—between Protestants and Catholics, for example, or to use the American example, between white and black workers. It can raise fundamental political questions about how society is run: "Do the Unionists really look after working-class Protestants?" for instance, or "Can Irish nationalism bring real change for ordinary Catholics?" And crucially, economic struggle like that waged in 1932 can create the kind of polarization necessary for socialist politics to emerge, as the development of the RWGs attested. "The political struggle periodically fertilises the ground for the economic struggle," as Rosa Luxemburg argued. "Cause and effect interchange every second."[9]

Class struggle, then, is a "self-changing" process: when workers fight together, as in 1932, they can re-alter the political landscape and in doing so re-create themselves.[10] Consider how quickly and dramatically Belfast changed during the ODR struggle. Or how the political dynamics of the city shifted, from outright communal hostility to a spirit of solidarity that permeated every cobbled street corner. In a matter of months Catholics and Protestants went from rioting against one another during the Eucharistic Congress in July 1932 to building barricades together a mere three months later. Working-class struggle like that which dominated the headlines in 1932 is, in essence, a process of becoming: a protracted sequence of illumination, where old habits are challenged and the working class can, through its own self-activity, become "a class for itself."[11] And the evidence for this is clear to see in the course of the ODR struggle, where previously estranged communities joined in battle against the RUC, sometimes with IRA men and B-Specials fighting on the same side, led by a relatively small band of revolutionary

Communists and in the end leading to significant concessions from the usually uncompromising Unionist government.

If this were the end of the story, of course, then the unity of 1932 would never have been defeated. The chief lesson of 1932 is not that class unity is impossible, but that the *process of becoming* that it creates will not progress uninterrupted or toward an inevitable socialist conclusion. In other words, 1932 opened up the possibility for a sustained class politics, but this opportunity had to be seized upon and organized into a political force, one that was capable of posing a counter-hegemonic alternative to the communal forces running the state. The pale ghosts of sectarianism, therefore, can retreat under the pressure of class unity, but they do not dissipate or disappear of their own accord. The lesson is in no way particular to politics in the North of Ireland. Commenting on the fortunes of the 1871 Paris Commune, history's first socialist experiment, Karl Marx spoke of how the revolutionary action is often stifled by the old order that it challenges:

> And just as they seem to be occupied with revolutionizing themselves and things, creating something that did not exist before, precisely in such epochs of revolutionary crisis they anxiously conjure up the spirits of the past to their service, borrowing from them names, battle slogans, and costumes in order to present this new scene in world history in time-honored disguise and borrowed language.[12]

In Belfast between 1932 and 1935, as in Paris in 1871, the spirits of the past were conjured up to great effect. In commenting about the Paris Commune, Marx never intended to argue that workers were incapable of abandoning old ideas, what he called the "muck of ages." His point was instead to stress that the process of overcoming these ideas was not inevitable, and it would be challenged by ruling-class agitation. In any struggle, therefore, including that of 1932, some people will draw socialist conclusions and some will not. But for the most part, working-class people will have what Engels called "contradictory consciousness": the ideas they carry into confrontation with the old order will be a combination of those that they have inherited from society and the ideas that they have learned in struggle. The

Italian Marxist Antonio Gramsci developed this theory more systematically, arguing that the ideas that dominate inside the working-class movement could often be in complete contrast to its practice:

> The active person-in-the-mass has a practical activity, but has no clear theoretical consciousness of their practical activity . . . Their theoretical consciousness can indeed be historically in opposition to their activity. One might almost say they have two theoretical consciousnesses (or one contradictory consciousness); one which is implicit in their activity and which in reality unites them with all their fellow-workers in the practical transformation of the real world; and one, superficially explicit or verbal, which they have inherited from the past and uncritically absorbed.[13]

Why is this the case? As Gramsci suggests, consciousness is made up of two interrelated elements. On the one hand, people's ideas are influenced by the ideologies that dominate all around them. But they are also heavily influenced by their own day-to-day experience. In a segregated society like Northern Ireland, sectarian ideas can, even in a convoluted way, match people's experience: this is why sectarianism continues to persist, even when it often clashes with the interests of those who follow it. When Catholics and Protestants struggle together, however—as they did during the ODR dispute—much of this segregated experience can be overcome, the reality of sectarian ignorance challenged, and socialist ideas argued for anew. Gramsci suggests, however, that socialist ideas cannot win through spontaneous action alone. Instead, there must be a "struggle of political 'hegemonies' and of opposing directions."[14] For anti-sectarian, socialist ideas to grow they must become organized, to become a "material force," as Marx argued.

For much of the history of the labor movement in Belfast, however, class struggle has emerged without any organization capable of arguing clear socialist, anti-sectarian politics, leaving the movement susceptible to the intervention of forces articulating a reactionary and sectarian perspective. This was the experience during the Dockers' Strike of 1907, for example, and that of the General Strike of 1919, when virtually no serious organization existed that consistently espoused socialist politics. In 1932, however, the basis for such an organization did exist in the form of the RWGs. The problem was that it did not combine its obvious practical achievements with the building of a network of militants in working-class communities capable of both organizing an economic strike *and* raising a political fight against sectarianism. It is not a simple question, therefore, of creating a link between ideas and action. Rather, we must develop a synthesis of the two. As I have written elsewhere: "Revolutionary action, [as Marx put it], must be 'practical-critical.' That is to say it must combine a practical engagement with the building of real struggle with an ideological offensive against bourgeois ideas. The history of the Left in the North, unfortunately, is the history of the separation of these two things."[15] The lesson for the labor movement in the midst of the Great Depression, therefore, is as profound as it is simple: you can ignore sectarianism, but sectarianism won't ignore you. Even if workers do unite, which they invariably will, if sectarian ideas are left unchallenged, then reactionary forces will reorganize and eventually divide the class once more, "I wasted time," as Richard II warned, "And now doth time waste me."

Belfast is today a city burdened by the ghosts of its past, with the imagery of various historical events adorning countless gable walls throughout its streets and housing estates. On these increasingly tourist-driven trails, however, there is little reference to the ODR struggle; there are no statues, no plaques, and no murals dedicated to the event. Certainly the story of Bloody Tuesday (as it was known to locals at the time) survived in local lore, and word of mouth would keep the story alive for years to come, particularly within the small and often isolated networks of left-wing activism. Historical memory can, however, be fleeting. Past events tend to survive in popular consciousness only when forces in the present choose to preserve them, and neither the state-funded tourism industry nor any of the major political forces in the North of Ireland—namely unionism and nationalism—has any stake in preserving the memory of the working-class unity of 1932.

The experience of the ODR struggle cannot be completely vanquished, however. Its legacy remains as a reminder that the possibility for workers' unity is out there, somewhere. Perhaps the most pertinent question to ask, then, is whether this chapter in our past can repeat itself in the present. Could Belfast once more rumble to the sounds of a united workers' movement in the way that it did in 1932? It has certainly been a long wait, and the circumstances are unlikely to be repeated in exact form. Some might suggest that this is precisely the point: that 1932 was a unique situation, created by the terrible economic conditions of the Depression era, that the sheer misery, hunger, and degradation of the period forced Protestant and Catholics to come together momentarily. Desperate times, after all, call for desperate measures.

It is true that the working classes of the 1930s were entrapped in the most inhumane and life-threatening of circumstances. And though Belfast today is far from heaven on earth—with widespread unemployment and a low-wage economy—the poverty of 1932 and the poverty in the city today are hardly like-for-like. It is folly to think, however, that class unity can only remerge when the days of abject starvation return. In truth, struggle is not dictated by levels and degrees of absolute poverty but rather by the expectations of working-class people. Capitalism is a dynamic system, and in periods of growth the expectations can rise. But the contradictions of the system—as in the Great Depression of the 1930s—continuously force it into conflict with the interests of those whose exploitation lies at the heart of modern capitalism. The particular convergence of circumstances that can generate an outburst of class discontent is specific to a given historical period, but struggle does inevitably arise. When the expectations of working-class people clash with the interests of the system, the conditions for struggle emerge.

A more serious objection to the relevance of 1932 is the entrenched nature of sectarianism today. This seems, on the surface, to be an obvious obstacle. Northern Ireland remains a deeply divided society. While chronic sectarian violence has reduced significantly from its peak during the protracted period of conflict known as the Troubles, the effects of the conflict continue to scar the population and to sour prospects for a future unmarked by division. Sectarianism is now enshrined and institutionalized into the very fabric of the political system. The "power sharing" arrangement at the heart of the Belfast Agreement—whereby political representatives in the Assembly at Stormont must identify as "Nationalist" or "Unionist," with very little space left for those who might identify as "other"— has institutionalized sectarianism to such a degree that bigoted practices and traditions are normalized and even protected by the state.

Some things have changed, however. It is true that today the ability of the state to give preference to one side over the other— as the Unionist government sought to do through discrimination against Catholics for much of its existence—has been greatly reduced. In its place, however, is the institutionalization of the kind of political discourse promoted by groups like the Ulster Protestant League in the 1930s but now accepted as normal inside the Northern Ireland Assembly: that the advancement of one side can only come at the expense of the other. According to its architects, the Belfast Agreement was designed to bridge the historical gap between unionism and nationalism. A decade and a half after its signing, however, the balance sheet does not appear to have confirmed this prediction; the so-called Agreement has not led to a decline in sectarian animosity but, paradoxically, to its intensification.

We have seen enough of the "new" Northern Ireland to be able to conclude that the society born from the Belfast Agreement has not managed to move beyond persistent and chronic sectarianism. Time and time again this has been manifest in the emergence of vicious sectarian agitation on the streets. In recent memory this took the form of the "flag protests" which began in 2012. These brought hundreds and occasionally more than a thousand loyalists out onto the streets to demand that the Union Jack be flown on top of Belfast City Hall 365 days of the year, often disrupting day-to-day life in Belfast. But this was not the only time that communal conflict has remerged. On a number of occasions, including the Orange Order–led siege of Garvaghy Road in the late 1990s, the loyalists' picketing of the Holy Cross girls school in 2001, loyalist-orchestrated street protests in 2006, or the episodic confrontations around Ardoyne in North Belfast and the Short Strand in East Belfast, the potential for a return to bitter sectarian conflict has revealed itself on the streets of the city. It does not help that there are forces on the republican side who continue to harbour illusions that the solution lies in a return to an armed conflict. Although the so-called "dissident threat" is never far from the headlines, support for such an approach is neg-ligible—even within the most socially deprived nationalist commu-nities. Far from challenging the status quo or offering an alternative to Sinn Féin's embrace of the establishment, militarism strengthens the hand of the state, reinforcing sectarian division in the process.

Hope, however, remains—even amid the failure of the Belfast Agreement to deliver real change. While no real or sustainable solu-tion to sectarian division is likely to emerge from the sectarian carve-up dominated by Unionist and Nationalist elites, important signs of a new politics have emerged. In 2006, hundreds of postal workers from both sides of the community took wildcat strike action. In echoes of 1932, they marched up the Shankill and down the Falls, conscious no doubt that sectarian forces would seek to divide them. The strike was small, but it was a signal that workers could unite. In November 2011, and again in March 2015, tens of thousands of Catholics and Protestant public sector workers took strike action against austerity. While neither strike was as sustained or as militant as that in 1932, they did indicate that the power of the working class was far from dead. Nor has the socialist Left in Northern Ireland been completely vanquished either. The emergence of People Before Profit—a 32-county socialist party with elected representation on both sides of the border—is a sign of this. Should developments like these have any serious hope of contributing to a wider resurgence of class politics then it must be able to combine two key elements: an understanding that it is only through class unity that workers can advance, and an insistence on the necessity of consistently challeng-ing sectarian ideas. This, in the end, is the incontestable lesson of the experience of 1932.

The weight of the past, as Marx reminds us, weighs heavily on the minds of the living. Nowhere is this truer than in Belfast, a city with more than its share of nightmares to dwell upon. In the long and bitter history of a sectarian state, however, there was an awak-ening: in one glorious moment in 1932, two estranged communities began to move toward common struggle, and in doing so planted the seeds for a new movement to grow. In bloom, it revealed the possibility of a united working class, illuminating the path less trodden in Irish politics: of class over creed, of solidarity in struggle, of a socialist future. That it was trampled on before it could fully flower was neither an outcome determined beforehand by historical inevitability nor a result of incompatible cultural identities, but the end result of an intense and unequal political struggle between defenders of the old order and harbingers of a better world, whose final defeat could have been avoided. The struggle of 1932 is long gone, but the seeds of working-class unity remain, and under the right circumstances they can sprout once more. If the history of all existing society is the history of class struggle, then we can say with some confidence that the final chapter in Belfast has yet to be written.

ACKNOWLEDGMENTS

This book has been five years in the making. That is not to say it took five years to write—the majority of it was finished some time ago. Life itself, however, has a way of interrupting the writing process, particularly when you are preparing it in your spare time, as I was with this study. The twin curses of perfectionism and procrastination did not speed up the process either, though I hope the reader appreciates the effort made to make this book as lively and readable as possible, whatever imperfections may remain.

I must begin by thanking Anthony Arnove at Haymarket Books, who believed in this project from the start, was helpful and supportive throughout, and has the patience of a saint. A tip of the hat to St. Arnove, therefore, for seeing this project through to completion. I can only hope the wait was worth it. Dao X. Tran's persistence made sure the book was completed and her expert management of the editorial process ensured it came out in the best possible shape. The entire team at Haymarket was extremely professional, and it was a pleasure to work with a publisher that cares as much about the production of good books as it does about the dissemination of progressive politics. Thanks as well to Jessie Kindig and Brian Baughan for their work on the manuscript.

This book greatly benefited from people who read it or were forced to endure me talking about it at great length. Mike Davis, Paul Laverty, Ken Loach, Eamonn McCann, and Mike Milotte all kindly took time out of their busy schedules to read the book and to provide blurbs. My enthusiasm for the ODR riots is perhaps only matched by that of Martin Lynch, and I greatly appreciated the long conversations we had about the topic during work on *The People of Gallagher Street*. Thanks as well to Kieran Allen, Shaun Harkin, Joseph Ferran, Fiona Ferguson, Fearghal Mac Bhloscaidh, Séamus Mac Seáin, Bríd Smith, and "Dan Bear" Quinn for either reading or discussing the book with me. Matt Collins spent long hours, sometimes into the early hours of the night, discussing the book and its contents with me over the last few years. To this end, Matt would like to thank the staff of the Casement, Devenish, Whitefort, and Hunting Lodge for their assistance in this endeavor.

Special mention must go to Brian Kelly. Very few people can rely on a Deutscher prize–winning historian to assist them in the production of a book. Still fewer could expect any full-time historian to devote the kind of time and energy that Brian did to this work, both in discussion with me, and more importantly in his meticulous and sometimes brutal copyediting. I was delighted when he agreed to write the foreword.

I would like to thank my parents Seán and Cathy, my brother Aodán and sister Aoife, and my wider family. Wendy Ní Fhionn was my rock throughout. I could not have done it without her.

NOTES

Foreword

1. As Mitchell acknowledges, the collection of oral histories on the Depression years by Ronaldo Munck and Bill Rolston in *Belfast in the Thirties: An Oral History* (New York: St. Martin's Press, 1987) constitutes an important act of historical recovery, without which a reconstruction of the ODR strike would be far more difficult. The present study offers a critical analysis of those events beyond the scope of that valuable work.

2. James Connolly, *Labour in Irish History* (New York: Donnelly Press, 1919), 14; Henry Patterson, *Class Conflict and Sectarianism: The Protestant Working Class and the Labour Movement, 1860–1920* (Belfast: Blackstaff Press, 1980), x.

3. On the link between nineteenth-century industrial transformation, changing demography and rising sectarian tensions, see Emrys Jones, *The Social Geography of Belfast* (Oxford University Press, 1960), 189–92; A. T. Q. Stewart, *The Narrow Ground: Patterns of Ulster History* (Belfast: Pretani Press, 1986), 143–44, 152; Brian Lamkin, Patrick Fitzgerald and Johanne Devlin Trew, "Migration in Belfast History: Trajectories, Letters, Voices," in Olwen Purdue, ed. *Belfast: The Emerging City, 1850–1914* (Dublin: Irish Academic Press, 2013), 235–70; S. J. Connolly and Gillian McIntosh, "Whose City? Belonging and Exclusion in the Nineteenth-Century Urban World," in S. J. Connolly, ed. *Belfast 400: People, Place and History* (Liverpool: Liverpool University Press, 2012), 245–55; A. C. Hepburn, "Work, Class and Religion in Belfast, 1871–1911," in Hepburn, *A Past Apart: Studies in the History of Catholic Belfast, 1850–1950* (Belfast: Ulster Historical Foundation, 1996), 68–87; Patterson, *Class Conflict and Sectarianism*, xvii, 25, 28–29, 115; Paul Bew, "Politics and the Rise of the Skilled Working Man," in J. C. Beckett, ed. *Belfast: The Making of the City, 1800–1914* (Belfast: Appletree Press, 1983), 136; Andrew Boyd, *The Rise of the Irish Trade Unions, 1729–1970* (Tralee: Anvil Books, 1972), 10, 75. Catherine Hirst exonerates Belfast's leading employers from involvement in promoting division and argues—in a similar vein to Patterson, and against the grain of Mitchell's argument here—that "[s]ectarianism was a working-class phenomenon." See Hirst, *Religion, Politics and Violence in Nineteenth-Century Belfast: The Pound and Sandy Row* (Dublin: Four Courts Press, 2002), 34.

4. John Gray, *City in Revolt: James Larkin and the Belfast Dock Strike of 1907* (Belfast: Blackstaff Press, 1985).

5. Patterson, *Class Conflict and Sectarianism*, 92–114; Conor Kostick, *Revolution in Ireland: Popular Militancy, 1917–1923* (London: Pluto Press, 1996), 51–69;

Emmett O'Connor, *Syndicalism in Ireland, 1917–1923* (Cork: Cork University Press, 1988), 71–73. The best analysis of this important strike—now out of print—appears in Michael Farrell, "The Great Belfast Strike of 1919," *Northern Star* 3 (February–March 1971). Patterson offers a contrasting assessment emphasizing the immutability of unionist ideology among Protestant strikers.

6.   Useful fragments on Belfast's linen industry and the role of female labor in it can be found in D. L. Armstrong, "Social and Economic Conditions in the Belfast Linen Industry, 1850–1900," *Irish Historical Studies* 7, no. 28 (1950–51): 235–269; Patterson, *Class Conflict and Sectarianism*, xiii, 24–25, 29–32, 37–38; Denise Kleinrichert, "Labour and Suffrage—Spinning Threads in Belfast," in Louise Ryan and Margaret Ward, eds., *Irish Women and the Vote: Becoming Citizens* (Dublin: Irish Academic Press, 2007), 189–208; Betty Messenger, *Picking Up the Linen Threads: Life in Ulster's Mills* (Belfast: Blackstaff Press, 1978).

7.   Recent studies that explore the function of rebranding in Belfast's post-conflict economy include Brian Kelly, "Neoliberal Belfast: Disaster Ahead?" *Irish Marxist Review* 1, no. 2 (2012): 44–59; Peter Shirlow, "Belfast: the 'Post-Conflict' City," *Space and Polity* 10, no. 2 (2006): 99–107; John Nagle, "Potemkin Village: Neo-liberalism and Peacebuilding in Northern Ireland?," *Ethnopolitics* 8, no. 2 (2009): 173–90; Colin Coulter, "Under Which Constitutional Arrangement Would You Still Prefer to Be Unemployed? Neoliberalism, the Peace Process, and the Politics of Class in Northern Ireland," *Studies in Conflict & Terrorism* 37, no. 9 (2014): 763–76.

8.   Jamie Smyth, "Northern Ireland Forges Ring of Steel to Protect G8 Summit," *Financial Times*, June 14, 2013; Kevin Magee, "G8: New Report Says Final Cost for Fermanagh Summit Was £92m," BBC News NI, January 23, 2015.

9.   Jasper Copping, "'Fake Shops' Open Up Ahead of the G8 Summit," *Telegraph*, May 31, 2013; Warren Hoge, "Icy Relations in Ulster Melt at the Hockey Games," *New York Times*, January 8, 2002; Helen Carson, "Tall Ships: Breaking Down Sectarian Barriers with the Tides of Change," *Belfast Telegraph*, July 2, 2015; Rebecca Black, "How Twitter Is Defusing Sectarian Tension," *Belfast Telegraph*, March 31, 2015.

10.   John Newsinger, *Fenianism in Mid-Victorian Britain* (London: Pluto Press, 1994), 84.

11.   Brian Hanley, "'Moderates and Peacemakers': Irish Historians and the Revolutionary Centenary," *Irish Economic and Social History* 43, no. 1 (2016): 117.

Introduction

Epigraph source: Royal Ulster Constabulary report, Public Record Office of Northern Ireland, Belfast, p. 4, HA/8/276.

1.   On the Ulster plantation and the violence attending colonization, see Jonathan Bardon, *A History of Ulster*, updated ed. (Belfast: Blackstaff Press, 2007), 115–47.

2.   Boyd, *The Rise of Irish Trade Unions*, 75.

3.   Paul Nolan, *Northern Ireland Peace Monitoring Report: Number Two* (Belfast: Community Relations Council, 2013), 87.

4. Paddy Devlin, *Yes, We Have No Bananas: Outdoor Relief in Belfast, 1920–1939* (Belfast: Blackstaff Press, 1981).
5. Ibid., 125.
6. Ronaldo Munck and Bill Rolston, with Gerry Moore, *Belfast in the Thirties: An Oral History* (New York: St. Martin's Press, 1988).
7. Ibid., 154–55.
8. Ibid., 7–8.
9. Matt Treacy, *The Communist Party of Ireland, 1921–2011* (Dublin: Brocaire Books, 2012), 38.
10. Uinseann MacEoin, *The IRA in the Twilight Years: 1923–1948* (Dublin: Argenta, 1997), 225.

Chapter 1: The Creation of the Northern Ireland State

1. Kostick, *Revolution in Ireland*, 8.
2. Michael Farrell, *Arming the Protestants: The Formation of the Ulster Special Constabulary and the Royal Ulster Constabulary, 1920–27* (London: Pluto Press, 1983), 3.
3. James Connolly, "Sinn Fein, Socialism and the Nation," *Irish Nation*, January 23, 1909.
4. Farrell, *Arming the Protestants*, 3.
5. Bardon, *A History of Ulster*, 416.
6. Gray, *City in Revolt*, 82.
7. Kostick, *Revolution in Ireland*, 54.
8. Ibid., 54.
9. Gray, *City in Revolt*, 207.
10. Fergal McCluskey, *Tyrone: The Irish Revolution, 1912–23* (Dublin: Four Courts Press, 2014), 134.
11. James Connolly, "Labour and the Proposed Partition of Ireland," *Irish Worker*, March 14, 1914.
12. Bardon, *A History of Ulster*, 471.
13. Patrick Buckland, *A History of Northern Ireland* (New York: Holmes & Meier, 1981), 50.
14. Austen Morgan, *Labour and Partition: The Belfast Working Class, 1905–1923* (London: Pluto Press, 1991), 265.
15. Craig was awarded a peerage in 1927 and was usually referred to as Lord Craigavon thereafter.
16. Kostick, *Revolution in Ireland*, 157.
17. Michael Farrell, *Northern Ireland: The Orange State* (London: Pluto Press, 1976), 63.
18. Kostick, *Revolution in Ireland*, 154.
19. Boyd, *The Rise of the Irish Trade Unions*, 95.
20. Graham S. Walker, *A History of the Ulster Unionist Party: Protest, Pragmatism and Pessimism* (Manchester, UK: Manchester University Press, 2004), 44.
21. Ronaldo Munck, *Ireland: Nation, State, and Class Struggle* (Boulder, CO: Westview Press, 1985), 38.

22. Farrell, *Arming the Protestants*, 277.
23. The best account of the development of the B-Specials is in Farrell, *Arming the Protestants*.
24. John Gray, *Thomas Carnduff: Life and Writings* (Belfast: Lagan Press/Fortnight Educational Trust, 1994), 22.
25. Bardon, *A History of Ulster*, 476.
26. Tim Pat Coogan, *Michael Collins: A Biography* (New York: Palgrave, 2002), 327.
27. George Gilmore, *The Irish Republican Congress* (Cork: The Cork Workers Club, 1974), 10.
28. Alan F. Parkinson and Eamon Phoenix, *Conflicts in the North of Ireland, 1900–2000: Flashpoints and Fracture Zones* (Dublin: Four Courts, 2010), 99.
29. Cited in David McKittrick and David McVea, *Making Sense of the Troubles: The Story of the Conflict in Northern Ireland* (Chicago: New Amsterdam, 2002), 16.
30. McCluskey, *Tyrone*, 130.
31. See Buckland, *A History of Northern Ireland*, 50–54.
32. Kostick, *Revolution in Ireland*, 157.
33. Devlin, *Yes, We Have No Bananas*, 52–53.
34. Ibid., 55.
35. McCluskey, *Tyrone*, 129.

Chapter 2: Unemployment and Relief in the North of Ireland

1. Michael Farrell, *The Poor Law and the Workhouse in Belfast, 1838–1948* (Belfast: Public Record Office of Northern Ireland, 1978), 1.
2. Ibid., 3.
3. Ibid., 1.
4. Friedrich Engels, *The Conditions of the Working Class in England*, ed. David McLellan, reissued ed. (London: Oxford University Press, 2009), 284–88.
5. F. S. L. Lyons, *Ireland since the Famine* (London: Fontana Press, 1985), 78.
6. Farrell, *Poor Law and the Workhouse in Belfast*, 76.
7. Maurice Goldring, *Belfast: From Loyalty to Rebellion* (London: Lawrence & Wishart, 1989), 48.
8. Farrell, *Poor Law and the Workhouse in Belfast*, 84.
9. Devlin, *Yes, We Have No Bananas*, 84.
10. Ibid., 81.
11. Ibid., 73.
12. *Irish News*, July 4, 1932.
13. Christopher Norton, "Creating Jobs, Manufacturing Unity: Ulster Unionism and Mass Unemployment, 1922–34," *Contemporary British History* 15, no. 2 (2001), 2.
14. Pierre-Vincent Moreau, "Poverty Relief and the Economic Crisis in the Region of Belfast from 1921 to 1939," prepared for the Public Records of Northern Ireland, August 2010, http://www.workhouses.org.uk/Belfast/moreau2.pdf, pp. 2–3.
15. Norton, "Creating Jobs," 6.
16. Farrell, *Northern Ireland*, 122.

17. Ibid., 122–23.
18. "Fisher Sees Stocks Permanently High," *New York Times*, October 16, 1929, 8.
19. For a fuller explanation of the Wall Street Crash, see Chris Harman, *Explaining the Crisis: A Marxist Reappraisal*, second printing (London: Bookmarks, 1987), 50–74.
20. *Belfast Newsletter*, October 26, 1929.
21. *Belfast Newsletter*, October 30, 1929.
22. *Belfast Telegraph*, October 31, 1929.
23. *Belfast Newsletter*, November 18, 1929.
24. *Belfast Newsletter*, November 4, 1929.
25. For more on this, see D. S. Johnson, "The Northern Ireland Economy, 1914–39," in Líam Kennedy and Philip Ollerenshaw, eds., *An Economic History of Ulster, 1820–1939* (Manchester: Manchester University Press, 1985), 184–88.
26. Bardon, *A History of Ulster*, 523.
27. Munck and Rolston, *Belfast in the Thirties*, 126.
28. Bardon, *A History of Ulster*, 526.
29. Gray, *Thomas Carnduff*, 105–6.
30. Johnson, "Northern Ireland Economy."
31. Munck and Rolston, *Belfast in the Thirties*, 19.
32. Ibid., 65.
33. Devlin, *Yes, We Have No Bananas*, 11.
34. Norton, "Creating Jobs," 4.
35. For an account of the shifting strategies of Unionist elites, see Paul Bew and Christopher Norton, "The Unionist State and the Outdoor Relief Riots of 1932," *Economic and Social Review* 10, no. 3 (1979), 255–65.
36. Buckland, *A History of Northern Ireland*, 75.
37. For an account of some of these struggles, see Wal Hannington, *Unemployed Struggles, 1919–1936: My Life and Struggles amongst the Unemployed* (New York: Barnes & Noble Books, 1973).
38. *Irish News*, July 19, 1932.
39. John Steinbeck, *The Grapes of Wrath*, Penguin Modern Classics ed. (1939; Harmondsworth, UK: Penguin Books, 1962), 217.

Chapter 3: The Unemployed Get Organized

1. Farrell, *Northern Ireland: The Orange State*, 124.
2. Devlin, *Yes, We Have No Bananas*, 117.
3. Ibid., 121.
4. Munck and Rolston, *Belfast in the Thirties*, 87.
5. James Kelly, *Bonfires on the Hillside: An Eyewitness Account of Political Upheaval in Northern Ireland* (Belfast: Fountain, 1995), 66.
6. Ibid., 67.
7. Letter to Belfast Corporation, 3 November 1932, file: "Employment," Public Record Office of Northern Ireland (PRONI), Belfast, Local Authorities (LA) papers, LA/7/3/A/7.
8. Bardon, *A History of Ulster*, 531.

9.   Ibid., 531.
10. Medical Superintendent Officer of Health, report on Health in Belfast, 1932, Reports of Medical Officer of Health (DA), PRONI LA/7/9/DA/26.
11. Gray, *Thomas Carnduff*, 105.
12. Ibid., 29.
13. Thomas Carnduff, *Songs of an Out-of-Work* (Belfast: Quota Press, 1932), 23–24.
14. Letter to Belfast Corporation by Joseph Catherwood, 19 August 1932, file: "Employment," PRONI LA/7/3/A/7.
15. Letter from Mr. David Eakin of Broom Street on the Shankill Road to the Lord Mayor, 4 July 1932, file: "Employment," PRONI LA/7/3/A/7.
16. Letter to Sir Crawford McCullough, acknowledged 23 November 1932, file: "Employment," PRONI LA/7/3/A/7.
17. See file: "Employment," PRONI LA/7/3/A/7.
18. *Irish News*, July 16, 1932.
19. Cited in Munck and Rolston, *Belfast in the Thirties*, 23.
20. Emmet O'Connor, *James Larkin* (Radical Irish Lives) (Cork: Cork University Press, 2002), 87.
21. Emmet O'Connor, "Bolshevising Irish Communism: The Communist International and the Formation of the Revolutionary Workers' Groups, 1927–31," *Irish Historical Studies* 33, no. 132 (2003), 453.
22. Treacy, *Communist Party of Ireland*, 32.
23. O'Connor, "Bolshevising Irish Communism," 462.
24. "Circulation of Worker's Voice," 25 August 1932, Russian State Archive of Socio-Political History (RGASPI), Moscow, 495/89/84.
25. Letter from Belfast County Grand Lodge Lord Mayor, 28 May 1932, PRONI LA/7/3A/5.
26. Buckland, *A History of Northern Ireland*, 71.
27. Mike Milotte, *Communism in Modern Ireland: The Pursuit of a Workers' Republic since 1916* (Dublin: Gill and Macmillan, 1984), 127.
28. Letter from the Inspector General's Office to the Ministry of Home Affairs, 20 October 1930, Ministry of Home Affairs (HA) papers, PRONI HA/32/1/544.
29. Letter from the Inspector General's Office to the Ministry of Home Affairs, 9 February 1931, PRONI HA/32/1/544; Letter from the Inspector General's Office to the Ministry of Home Affairs, 9 March 1931, PRONI HA/32/1/544; Letter from the Inspector General's Office to the Ministry of Home Affairs, 5 January 1931, PRONI HA/32/1/544.
30. Report from the Inspector General's Office to the Ministry of Home Affairs (titled "Irish Unemployed Workers Meeting"), 2 April 1930, PRONI HA/32/1/544.
31. Kelly, *Bonfires on the Hillside*, 69.
32. Police file on Tommy Geehan, PRONI HA/5/1304.
33. Tommy Geehan's "Cadre File" from Lenin School, 1930, RGASPI, 495/218/15.
34. Letter from Inspector General to Ministry of Home Affairs, Royal Ulster Constabulary (RUC) file on Tommy Geehan, 8 September 1927, PRONI HA/5/1304.

35. For a selection of Tommy Geehan's articles in this period, see the entries on the South Belfast Constituency Labour Party in Joe Keenan, ed., *"The Labour Opposition in Northern Ireland": Complete Reprint of the First Labour Newspaper in Northern Ireland, 1925–26* (Belfast: Athol Books, 1992)

36. Reports on activities of Workers' Defence League, Irish National Unemployed Workers' Movement and Communist Activity, PRONI, HA/32/1/544; Tommy Geehan "Cadre File," RGASPI, 495/218/15.

37. Transcript of speech given by Betty Sinclair in the 1950s, quoted in "Belfast's October," collected in Sean Nolan, ed., *Communist Party of Ireland: Outline History* (Belfast: New Books Publications, 1975), 55.

38. Kelly, *Bonfires on the Hillside*, 69.

39. *Irish Workers' Voice*, July 2, 1932.

40. Ibid.

41. Ibid.

42. *Irish News*, August 4, 1932.

43. Report of Outdoor Relief Committee, 9 August 1932, minutes of Board of Guardians, pp. 327–29, BG 7/A/128.

44. *Irish Workers' Voice*, August 20, 1932.

45. Ibid.

46. Police report on "Communist and Relief Workers Demonstration," 19 August 1932, PRONI HA/8/276.

47. *Irish Workers' Voice*, August 27, 1932.

48. *Belfast Newsletter*, August 19, 1932.

49. *Irish Workers' Voice*, August 27, 1932.

50. Letter from Seán Murray, September 9, 1932, RGASPI 495/89/83-84.

51. *Irish Workers' Voice*, September 10, 1932.

52. Police report on "Belfast Outdoor Relief Workers Demonstration & Meeting," p. 1, 1 September 1932, PRONI HA/8/276.

53. Ibid., 1–2.

54. *Irish Workers' Voice*, September 10, 1932.

55. Ibid.

56. Malachy Gray, "A Shop Steward Remembers," *Saothar* 11 (1986): 111.

57. Police report on "Belfast Outdoor Relief Workers Demonstration & Meeting," p. 7, 1 September 1932, PRONI HA/8/276.

58. See *Belfast Telegraph*, September 2–3, 1932.

59. On the Whiterock demonstration, see the police report on "Outdoor Relief Workers Meeting at Whiterock Crescent," 16 September 1932, PRONI HA/8/276. The Newtonards rally is discussed in "Outdoor Relief Workers Meeting at Junction of Templemore Avenue and Newtonards Road," September 9, 1932, PRONI HA/8/276.

60. Letter to Comintern from RWGs, 28 November 1932, RGASPI 459/89/84.

61. Report of Outdoor Relief Committee, 23 August 1932, minutes of Board of Guardians, pp. 449–51, Board of Guardians (BG), PRONI BG 7/A/128.

62. Report of Outdoor Relief Committee, 6 September 1932, minutes of Board of Guardians, pp. 573–74, BG 7/A/128.

63. Ibid., pp. 705–10.
64. Ibid., 701–3.
65. Angela Clifford, *Poor Law in Ireland: With an Account of the Belfast Outdoor Relief Dispute, 1932, and the Development of the British Welfare State, and Social Welfare in the Republic* (Belfast: Athol Books, 1983), 13.
66. All quotes from *Belfast Telegraph*, September 30, 1932, 15.
67. *Irish News*, September 30, 1932, 5.
68. All quotes in this and preceeding paragraph from *Belfast Newsletter*, September 30, 1932.
69. Police report to Ministry for Home Affairs: "Belfast Outdoor Relief Workers Meeting," 23 September 1932, PRONI HA/8/276.
70. *Belfast Telegraph*, September 30, 1932.
71. Police report on "Outdoor Relief Workers Meeting at Grosvenor Minor Hall," 27 September 1932, PRONI HA/8/276.
72. *Irish News*, September 30, 1932.

Chapter 4: The Outdoor Relief Strike

1. Munck and Rolston, *Belfast in the Thirties*, 27.
2. Speech given by Betty Sinclair in the 1950s, in Nolan, *Communist Party of Ireland*, 55.
3. *Belfast Telegraph*, October 4, 1932.
4. *Irish News*, October 4, 1932.
5. The smallest estimate came from the RUC, who said 30,000 attended. They noted however that at least 10,000 marched from East Belfast alone. RUC Report on "Relief Workers Demonstration," 4 October 1932, p. 1, PRONI HA/8/276.
6. *Belfast Newsletter*, October 4, 1932.
7. Ibid.
8. Invergordon, a town in Scotland, had been the scene of a mass mutiny in the Royal Navy the previous year.
9. RUC Report on "Relief Workers Demonstration," 4 October 1932, pp. 1–2, PRONI Ref HA/8/276.
10. Ibid., p. 2.
11. Kelly, *Bonfires on the Hillside*, 69–70.
12. Communication between RUC and Ministry of Home Affairs, 3 October 1932, PRONI HA/8/276.
13. Hazel Morrissey, *Betty Sinclair: A Woman's Fight for Socialism* (Belfast: Crescent Arts Cooperative, 1983).
14. *Belfast Telegraph*, October 5, 1932.
15. *Irish Independent*, October 5, 1932.
16. Report of Outdoor Relief Committee, 4 October 1932, minutes of Board of Guardians, pp. 858–69, BG 7/A/128.
17. *Irish News*, October 5, 1932; *Belfast Telegraph*, October 4, 1932.
18. *Irish News*, October 5, 1932.
19. *Belfast Telegraph*, October 3, 1932.
20. *Belfast Telegraph*, October 5, 1932.

21. Police report on "Meeting in St. Mary's Hall on 7th October 1932," p. 1, PRONI HA/8/276.
22. *Belfast Telegraph*, October 6, 1932; *Irish News*, October 6, 1932.
23. *Irish Independent*, October 6, 1932.
24. Police report on "Single Unemployed Men's Meeting at Templemore Avenue," p. 2, 6 October 1932, PRONI HA/9/276.
25. Reports of these riots can be found in *Irish News*, October 6, 1932.
26. Munck and Rolston, *Belfast in the Thirties*, 28.
27. Police report on "Single Unemployed Men's Meeting at Templemore Avenue," 6 October 1932, PRONI HA/9/276.
28. From a speech by RWG leader Arthur Griffin, contained in a police report on "Meeting in St. Mary's Hall on 7th October 1932," PRONI HA/8/276.
29. Farrell, *Poor Law and the Workhouse in Belfast,* 90.
30. "Belfast Union—Report of Emergency Committee," 7 October 1932, minutes of Board of Guardians, p. 889, BG 7/A/128.
31. "Belfast Union Report," 8 October 1932, minutes of Board of Guardians, p. 903, BG 7/A/128.
32. *Irish Independent,* October 7, 1932.
33. *Irish News,* October 7, 1932.
34. Ibid.
35. *Belfast Telegraph,* October 7, 1932.
36. Ibid.
37. Police report to Ministry of Home Affairs, "Meeting in St. Mary's Hall on 7th October 1932," PRONI HA/8/276.
38. Ibid.
39. Ibid., p. 3.
40. Ibid.
41. Ibid., p. 2.
42. *Belfast Telegraph*, October 8, 1932.
43. Police report to Ministry of Home Affairs, "Meeting in St. Mary's Hall on 7th October 1932," PRONI HA/8/276.
44. *Irish News,* October 10, 1932.
45. Farrell, *Northern Ireland,* 127.
46. Munck and Rolston, *Belfast in the Thirties,* 29.
47. For more on the unemployed movement in Derry, see Máirtín Ó Catháin, "'Struggle or Starve': Derry Unemployed Workers' Movements, 1926–35," *Saothar* 28 (2003): 49–60.
48. *Irish Independent,* October 5, 1932.
49. *Irish Independent,* October 6, 1932.
50. *Irish Independent,* October 12, 1932.
51. Letter to Comintern, November 28, 1932, RGASPI, 495/89/84.
52. *Belfast Newsletter,* October 5, 1932.
53. *Belfast Telegraph,* October 10, 1932.
54. Milotte, *Communism in Modern Ireland,* 130.
55. Kelly, *Bonfires on the Hillside,* 71–72.

56. *Irish News*, October 10, 1932.
57. Police report on "Meeting in St. Mary's Hall on 7th October 1932,", PRONI HA/8/276.
58. *Irish News*, October 11, 1932.
59. Munck and Rolston, *Belfast in the Thirties*, 30.
60. *Belfast Telegraph*, October 10, 1932.

Chapter 5: The ODR Riots: Belfast's "Festival of the Oppressed"

1. For reports of events on the evening of October 10, see *Irish News*, October 11, 1932; *Belfast Telegraph*, October 11, 1932.
2. *Belfast Telegraph*, October, 11, 1932.
3. Report of the trial of Maurice Watters can be found in *Belfast Telegraph*, October 11, 1932.
4. *Irish Independent*, October 12, 1932.
5. *Belfast Telegraph*, October 11, 1932.
6. Kelly, *Bonfires on the Hillside*, 74.
7. *Belfast Telegraph*, October 11, 1932.
8. *Irish News*, October 12, 1932.
9. *Belfast Telegraph*, January 31, 1933. Ramsey was later awarded a small amount of compensation, though the judge argued that the bullet must have come from the rioters. This was the explanation given by the police in other compensation cases after the riots. If this were the case, then we would have to believe that the rioters had shot seventeen of their own while failing to land a single bullet against the police.
10. MacEoin, *IRA in the Twilight Years*, 691.
11. Devlin, *Yes, We Have No Bananas*, 130.
12. Ibid.
13. Uinseann MacEoin, ed., *Harry: The Story of Harry White* (Dublin: Argenta, 1985), 36–37.
14. Kelly, *Bonfires on the Hillside*, 72–73.
15. Cited in Devlin, *Yes, We Have No Bananas*, 129; and Munck and Rolston, *Belfast in the Thirties*, 31.
16. *Irish News*, October 12, 1932.
17. Letter to Comintern, November 28, 1932, RGASPI, 495/89/84.
18. *Irish News*, October, 12, 1932.
19. *Irish Independent*, October 12, 1932.
20. *Irish News*, October 12, 1932.
21. From a letter written by Robert Morrow, 1932, in the Trade Union Records, 1788–1983, PRONI D1050/6/C/3.
22. *Irish News*, October 12, 1932.
23. "Report on the Situation in Belfast and the Steps Taken to Develop Communist Youth Organisation," 4 November 1932, RGASPI, 533/10/13.
24. Munck and Rolston, *Belfast in the Thirties*, 176.
25. Ibid.
26. Ibid., 175.

27. Letter from IRA to Seán Murray, 9 October 1932, RGASPI, 495/89/83-44.
28. MacEoin, *Harry*, 36–37.
29. Ibid., 36.
30. Munck and Rolston, *Belfast in the Thirties*, 177.
31. Letter to Comintern, 28 October 1932, RGASPI, 495/89/84.
32. *Irish Independent*, October 11, 1932.
33. *Irish Independent*, October 12, 1932.
34. *Irish Workers' Voice*, October 20, 1932.
35. *Irish Independent*, October 12, 1932.
36. MacEoin, *IRA in the Twilight Years*, 690.
37. *Belfast Telegraph*, October 12, 1932.
38. *Irish Independent*, October 13, 1932.
39. *Irish Independent*, October 12, 1932.
40. Editorial, *Belfast Telegraph*, October 12, 1932.
41. *Belfast Telegraph*, October 13, 1932.
42. Report of Outdoor Relief Committee, 11 October 1932, minutes of Board of Guardians, pp. 945–51, BG 7/A/128.
43. Ibid., pp. 941–42.
44. *Belfast Telegraph*, October 12, 1932.
45. Milotte, *Communism in Modern Ireland*, 131.
46. *Belfast Telegraph*, October 12, 1932.
47. *Irish Independent*, October 14, 1932.
48. MacEoin, *IRA in the Twilight Years*, 423.
49. *Irish News*, February 1, 1933.
50. For a list of those shot during the riots, see Devlin, *Yes, We Have No Bananas*, 130–31.
51. *Belfast Telegraph*, October 13, 1932.
52. Munck and Rolston, *Belfast in the Thirties*, 32.
53. *Belfast Newsletter*, October 13, 1932.
54. Cited in Paul Bew and Christopher Norton, "The Unionist State and the Outdoor Riots of 1932," *Economic and Social Review* 10, no. 3 (1979): 262.
55. *Irish Workers' Voice*, October 15, 1932.
56. Letter to Comintern, 28 October 1932, RGASPI, 495/89/84.
57. Kelly, *Bonfires on the Hillside*, 69.
58. Speech given by Betty Sinclair in the 1950s, in Nolan, *Communist Party of Ireland*, 57.
59. Editorial, *Belfast Telegraph*, October 14, 1932; *Belfast Telegraph*, October 15, 1932.
60. In later meetings after the riots, Tommy Geehan would dispute this allegation.
61. *Belfast Telegraph*, October 12, 1932.
62. *Belfast Telegraph*, October 17, 1932.
63. See report in *Irish Workers' Voice*, October 22, 1932; *Irish Independent*, October 15, 1932.
64. Devlin, *Yes, We Have No Bananas*, 132–33.
65. *Belfast Telegraph*, October 15, 1932.

66. *Irish Workers' Voice*, October 22, 1932.
67. *Irish Independent*, October, 17, 1932.
68. Ibid.
69. Report by Inspector General's Office on "Meeting of the Outdoor Relief Workers," 17 October 1932, PRONI HA/8/276.

Chapter 6: Aftermath: Class, Sectarianism, and the Left

1. Milotte, *Communism in Modern Ireland*, 135–36.
2. "National Meeting of the RWGs," 9 December 1932, RGASPI, 495/89/82-14.
3. "Report on the Situation in Belfast and the Steps Taken to Develop Communist Youth Organisation," 4 November 1932, RGASPI, 533/10/13.
4. "Report from Inspector General of the RUC to Ministry of Home Affairs," 20 October 1932, PRONI HA/8/276.
5. "RUC Report on ODR Workers Meeting," 26 October 1932, PRONI HA/8/276.
6. Emmet O'Connor, *Reds and the Green: Ireland, Russia, and the Communist Internationals 1919–43* (Dublin: University College of Dublin Press, 2004), 184.
7. *Belfast Telegraph*, January 31, 1933.
8. Ibid.
9. For a report on the debate at the Belfast Corporation, see *Belfast Telegraph*, February 2, 1933.
10. *Belfast Telegraph*, February 1, 1933.
11. *Irish News*, February 1, 1933.
12. *Irish News*, February 4, 1933.
13. Ibid.
14. *Irish News*, February 3, 1933.
15. *Irish News*, February 21, 1933.
16. *Irish News*, February 24, 1933.
17. *Irish News*, February 13, 1933.
18. *Irish News*, February 27, 1933.
19. MacEoin, *IRA in the Twilight Years*, 424.
20. Farrell, *Northern Ireland*, 134.
21. "RUC Report on Mass Unemployed Meeting at Custom House Steps," March 15, 1933, PRONI HA/8/276.
22. Ibid.
23. *Belfast Telegraph*, February 7, 1933.
24. *Belfast Telegraph*, February 1, 1933.
25. *Irish News*, February 8, 1933.
26. *Irish News*, February 28, 1933.
27. *Irish News*, March 10, 1933.
28. *Irish News*, February 20, 1933.
29. *Irish News*, February 21, 1933.
30. O'Connor, *Reds and the Green*, 194.
31. Letter from Inspector General's Office to Ministry of Home Affairs, 7 November 1933, PRONI HA/32/1/606.

32. Jim Lane, *On the IRA: Belfast Brigade Area* (Cork: Cork Workers Club, 1972), 8.
33. Report sent to Comintern, 26 July 1933, RGASPI, 496/89/91.
34. Minute Sheet, Ministry of Home Affairs, 4 October 1934, PRONI HA/32/1/469.
35. *Belfast Newsletter*, January 10, 1935.
36. *Belfast Newsletter*, January 22, 1935.
37. Devlin, *Yes, We Have No Bananas*, 139.
38. Ibid.
39. Ibid., 140.
40. Walker, *History of the Ulster Unionist Party*, 964.
41. Devlin, *Yes, We Have No Bananas*, 138.
42. Walker, *History of the Ulster Unionist Party*, 964.
43. A. C. Hepburn, "The Belfast Riots of 1935," *Social History* 15, no. 1 (1990): 77.
44. Munck and Rolston, *Belfast in the Thirties*, 41.
45. Brian Hanley, *The IRA, 1926–1936* (Dublin: Four Courts Press, 2002), 151.
46. Brendan Anderson, ed., *Joe Cahill: A Life in the IRA* (Dublin: O'Brien Press, 2002), 24.
47. Ronald Munck, "Class and Religion in Belfast—A Historical Perspective," *Journal of Contemporary History* 20, no. 2 (1985): 255–56.
48. Hanley, *The IRA*, 151.
49. Henry Patterson, *The Politics of Illusion: A Political History of the* IRA (London: Serif, 1997) 64–65.
50. National Meeting of the RWGs, 9 December 1932, RGASPI, 495/89/82-14.
51. Report to Comintern, 26 July 1933, RGASPI 495/89/90.
52. Duncan Hallas, *The Comintern* (London: Bookmarks, 1985), 141.
53. Milotte, *Communism in Modern Ireland*, 156.
54. Patrick Byrne, *Memories of the Republican Congress* (London: Four Provinces Bookshop, undated),12.
55. Ibid.
56. Ibid.
57. Walker, *History of the Ulster Unionist Party*, 964.
58. Hepburn, "Belfast Riots," 80.
59. Kelly, *Bonfires on the Hillside*, 79–80.
60. A. C. Hepburn, *A Past Apart: Studies in the History of Catholic Belfast, 1850–1950* (Belfast: Ulster Historical Foundation, 1996), 188.
61. Hepburn, "A Past Apart," 189.
62. For Geehan's case, see *Belfast Telegraph*, August 18, 1935.
63. Milotte, *Communism in Modern Ireland*, 140.
64. For a detailed account of the riots, see Hepburn, "A Past Apart," 174–202.
65. Milotte, *Communism in Modern Ireland*, 140.
66. For an example of this perspective, see Seán Byers, *Seán Murray: Marxist-Leninist and Irish Socialist Republican* (Dublin: Irish Academic Press, 2015).
67. O'Connor, *Reds and the Green*, 236.
68. Kelly, *Bonfires on the Hillside*, 76.

Conclusion

1. Sean Montgomery, unpublished memoir, p. 30, cited in Jim McDermott, *Northern Divisions: The Old IRA and the Belfast Pogroms, 1920–22* (Belfast: Beyond the Pale, 2001), 234.
2. Ibid.
3. Ibid.
4. Tommy Geehan's "Cadre File" from Lenin School, 1930, RGASPI, 495/218/15.
5. Inspector General of the RUC, "West Belfast Labour Party Meeting at Peel Street," 5 September 1927, report to Ministry of Home Affairs, PRONI HA/5/1304.
6. All quotes from *Irish Democrat*, August 1, 1937.
7. Farrell, *Northern Ireland*, 14.
8. Gerry Adams, *The New Ireland: A Vision for the Future* (Dingle: Brandon, 2005), 57.
9. Tony Cliff, *Rosa Luxemburg* (1959), www.marxists.org/archive/cliff/works/1969/rosalux/3-masstrike.htm.
10. Karl Marx, "Theses on Feuerbach" (1845), www.marxists.org/archive/marx/works/1845/theses/theses.htm.
11. Karl Marx, "The Poverty of Philosophy" (1847), www.marxists.org/archive/marx/works/1847/poverty-philosophy.
12. Karl Marx, *The Eighteenth Brumaire of Louis Bonaparte* (1852), www.marxists.org/archive/marx/works/1852/18th-brumaire.
13. Antonio Gramsci, *Selections from the Prison Notebooks*, Quintin Hoare and Geoffrey Nowell-Smith, eds. (New York: International Publishers, 1971), 333.
14. Ibid.
15. Seán Mitchell, "The Permanent Crisis of 21st Century Ulster Unionism," *Irish Marxist Review* 3, no. 9 (2014): 42.

INDEX

"Passim" (literally "scattered") indicates
intermittent discussion of a topic
over a cluster of pages.

ABOUT HAYMARKET BOOKS

Haymarket Books is a nonprofit, progressive book distributor and publisher, a project of the Center for Economic Research and Social Change. We believe that activists need to take ideas, history, and politics into the many struggles for social justice today. Learning the lessons of past victories, as well as defeats, can arm a new generation of fighters for a better world. As Karl Marx said, "The philosophers have merely interpreted the world; the point, however, is to change it."

We take inspiration and courage from our namesakes, the Haymarket martyrs, who gave their lives fighting for a better world. Their 1886 struggle for the eight-hour day reminds workers around the world that ordinary people can organize and struggle for their own liberation.

For more information and to shop our complete catalog of titles, visit us online at www.haymarketbooks.org.

Also Available from Haymarket Books

BRICS: An Anticapitalist Critique
Edited and introduced by Patrick Bond and Ana Garcia

Europe in Revolt: Mapping the New European Left
Edited by Catarina Príncipe and Bhaskar Sunkara

A James Connolly Reader
Edited by Shaun Harkin, Preface by Mike Davis

Nation-States: Consciousness and Competition
Neil Davidson

Radical Unionism: The Rise and Fall of Revolutionary Syndicalism
Ralph Darlington

ABOUT THE AUTHOR

Seán Mitchell is a socialist and activist from Belfast. Born and raised in the Andersonstown area, Seán is a Gaeilgeoir and an active member of the Irish language community in Belfast. A founding member of People Before Profit, Seán was the first candidate to stand under the party's banner. He is the author of *A Rebel's Guide to James Connolly* (2016) and writes for the *Irish Marxist Review*.